THE REAL GOD
YOU NEED TO KNOW
HIS NAME IS
JESUS

KATHLEEN HOLLOP

INK START MEDIA
265 Eastchester Dr Ste 133 #102
High Point NC 27262

THE REAL GOD
YOU NEED TO KNOW
HIS NAME IS
JESUS

He is no longer a baby in a manger.

*HE IS THE LIVING,
RESURRECTED KING OF KINGS
AND LORD OF LORDS*

Kathleen Hollop

KATHLEEN HOLLOP

(INSIDE COVER)

Are you tired of church as usual? Are you tired of the lack of signs, wonders and miracles that should be happening in the churches today, and are not? Are you tired of the enemy of your soul beating you up emotionally, physically and spiritually?

Isn't it time to receive the Holy Spirit Baptism of Power and Anointing to "Fight the good fight of faith", be a "good soldier", in the army of God?" To be an Overcomer instead of a victim?

Isn't it time we read, study, memorize, and speak the Word of God into our situations, trust God, and see Him move Mightily? He is True to His Word to Perform it.

Isn't it time that we stand in the Authority of Jesus and in the Power of Holy Spirit to see and do the Greater Signs, Wonders, and Miracles that Jesus said we will do?

Isn't it time we see our Jesus give us total Victory over the devil, as we rise up and take a stand with and for Jesus? Isn't it time for the Body of Christ to Surrender Fully to Jesus, receive the Isaiah 60 Glory, and take Our Nation and the Nations of the World back to Christ? Isn't it Time?

(BOOK DEDICATION)

This Book is dedicated to the Real God of Heaven and earth, who I have been blessed to know , follow and serve. His Name is Jesus.

Without my Jesus, I would have had no future, no liberty, no freedom from fear of death, no genuine love, peace, forgiveness for my many sins, no joy, no reason for my existence and no eternal life in heaven. Religion didn't die on a cross for me. Jesus did. His Blood, (the Blood of God), was shed to redeem mankind back to Father God. The only sacrifice for sin acceptable to Father God is His only begotten Son's Blood shed on the cross for us.

John 3:16 "For God so loved the world that He gave His only begotten Son, that whosoever believes in Him, (Jesus), has everlasting life." Jesus is a love gift to us from Father God. Jesus (Yeshua), is a gift; but a gift has to be received and accepted to really belong to you. If you don't accept the gift of Salvation by receiving Jesus into your heart and life, you will not be saved. Vain "Religion" cannot save anyone. Jesus Saves.

Jesus Loves You. He died for your sins and mine on the cross so that we could be forgiven and have eternal life. Jesus said, "I am the way, the truth, and the life. No man comes to the Father but by me." The choice is yours to accept God's Love gift, or reject Him. Choose Jesus Today.

(FORWORD)

May this book be used Mightily by God the Holy Spirit, to enlighten the eyes, minds and hearts of those who have been deceived by Satan. May this book reveal God's Truths, from His Word, in such a way that people will be set free from deception, lies, half-truths, and Satan's wicked schemes and demonic plots to destroy them. God's Truth sets people free, restores their lives and heals their wounds.

May this book impart Biblical Truths in a way that you can grab onto them and apply them to your circumstances, families, marriages, and lives. Without Jesus, we cannot fight the devil and win. With Jesus, and armed with the Word of God, and the Holy Spirit, we can have Victory over the forces of hell.

Our God operates in the Supernatural. No one can understand the Supernatural Works of Almighty God with their natural minds or intellect. We need to just believe that the God who made the sun, moon, stars, planets, universe, seas, dry land, birds, fish, mammals, and human beings, just spoke these things into existence, and they were.

Read this book and see what God has done with me and through me. He can work His Miracles in you and through you also, if you believe in Jesus, are Holy Ghost Baptized, and led by the Spirit of God. The Power of God is available to us today. The same power that raised Jesus from the dead dwells in the believers in Christ today. We are not defeated once we are taught how to stand as the Army of God, Fight the good fight of faith, and lay hold on God's Promises.

We have God's Spiritual Weapons to stand against the devil and take the Victory, in Jesus Name. These weapons are listed in Ephesians Chapter 6. They will be discussed further in Chapter 5 of this book.

Our God is a God of Battles. We must Stand with Him and Battle for our nation, our God-given Constitution, our Families, Our Christian Heritage, our Freedoms, our Rights (we have no right to murder babies), Our Liberties and the very future of this Nation. The heart and soul of America, our children, our grandchildren and future generations are at stake. We must stand up now, fight the devil and His Wicked ideologies, and take this Nation and this World back to God.

(PROLOGUE)

There is a spiritual battle raging every day for the souls of mankind. The war is on! The battle is bigger than any physical war that has ever been fought on planet earth. It involves every person of every nation, kindred, race, and tongue.

It is a battle that began before there was time, as we know it...before the earth ever existed... before human beings ever were...

Most people are not even aware of this battle that rages in their own minds, emotions, hearts, feelings, wills and lives. The battle is a battle for their very souls and where they will spend eternity.

They go through their lives oblivious to the fact that they are a unique, special, one-of-a-kind creation of an Almighty God, who loves them.

The God of Heaven and Earth desires to reveal Himself to you. He desires a heart to heart love relationship with you. He desires that you repent of your sins, receive Him as your Savior, and be a part of His Spiritual Family forever (not only now), but in heaven, with Him, for all eternity.

The enemy of God and man (Satan), desires to lure you into destructive addictions to drugs, alcohol, sexual lusts, sexual perversions, fornications, adulteries, gayness, pornography, gambling, discouragement, anger, hopelessness, cross-dressing, transgender, sex change surgeries, woks, despair, fear, and other types of misery that war against your soul, body and spirit.

Satan wants to destroy your marriage, your family relationships, your parental rights, your freedom of speech, your rights to defend your home and family, your rights to speak your faith and stand against him and his media lies, etc. He wants to rob your ability to love, have joy and peace, enjoy your life, and follow God. He wants to destroy the Christian Faith and subject everyone to a Wicked Government , run by him. He wants to be your God.

Satan wants you to embrace the lies of Marxism, Communism, Socialism, Racism, CRT, BLM, KKK, Nazism, Darwinism, Evolution (the religion of atheism), secular humanism, Woks, and his other devices. Very few people realize that Hitler was a Darwinist. The idea that the weak deserve to die and a superior race needs to rise up, is

DEMONIC AS HELL. Hitler tried to destroy the Jews and anyone who was handicapped, or had any imperfection. He murdered millions of people. Stalin, Mussolini, Lenin, Karl Marx, Hitler, Darwin, etc.. were all Satanic mad-men.

Karl Marx was a Satanist who came up with the sick, twisted, ideologies of Communism and Socialism. CRT AND BLM are part of the thirteen points of Communism. If they can divide the people into racism and racial hatred, vaccinated vrs unvaccinated, young vrs old, etc...they can step in and take over our nation. We must stand together and demand these ideologies be taken out of our schools and colleges immediately. They are poisoning our youth to hate our free nation and to want the devil's take over. They are programming our college students to hate Israel and America and support terrorism and Communism. Parents need to put their children in trade schools and avoid todays colleges made up of Communist deans ,Communist professors, atheists and people who hate God. Parents need to home school their children or put them in Christian Schools that only employ real Christian teachers who teach the Bible and are living it.

Once these ideologies take over a nation, the average person has no rights or freedoms at all. The government becomes the dictator, the slave owner, the decider of what job you can have, where you can live, who you can talk to, where you can go, what you can speak or not speak, how many children you can have, etc... It becomes your God and Controls You and every aspect of your life. It doesn't care whether you like it or not. You are stuck in demonic misery, and slavery that you cannot oppose or stop. Anyone trying to oppose it or stop it, is quickly arrested, tortured, and murdered by the Communist Party. They may even harvest your organs while they murder you.

Communist China murdered it's college students for having a peaceful protest, against Communism. They were desiring freedom and liberty and justice for all. They were gunned down and murdered by the Communist Party. Anyone who escaped, was hunted down by the Communist Government, imprisoned, forced to do hard manual labor until they died, or were put to death immediately. Communism shows no genuine love, mercy or compassion for anyone. The devil is incapable of these things. His agents are just like him, hateful, violent, and unmerciful.

We must stop these Satanic ideologies now and take our nation back to God.

Hell is not a big party, as some very foolish people believe. It is a place of everlasting torment, in eternal flames, burning, but never being fully consumed. It is a place of horror, misery, and terror. Once there, a person has no escape. They are there forever separated from God and everything wonderful, beautiful and lovely.

There is no beauty in hell. Since every good and perfect gift comes from God, there are no birds, no sunsets, no flowers, no plush gardens, no water to quench their thirst, no natural beauty, no hope, no love, no peace, no joy, no goodness, etc... They forsook God's Plan of Salvation through the Lord and Savior Jesus Christ and died in their sins. They are paying for their sins themselves, in hell.

The Bible says that hell is in the nethermost part of the earth. It is called the pit, the center of the earth etc.. Hollywood came up with a movie that showed the center of the earth with plush gardens, lakes, birds singing, flowers, etc...It was a ridiculous lie. The Bible says that Pharoah and his multitudes went down to hell. (You remember the Story of Moses). Pharoah and his army drowned in the sea and went down to hell. Their souls are in hell. Hell is a real place. Jesus spoke of it often.

Ridiculous Hollywood movies blaspheme Jesus Christ by accusing him of sin. If Jesus Christ did even one sin, he would not have been qualified to redeem fallen mankind. The lamb of God had to be a perfect lamb, without blemish or spot. Jesus led a perfect life. He did no sin, neither was any guile in his mouth. DaVinci Lies.

Hollywood's lies say that everyone is a child of God, everyone goes to heaven, no matter what they do or what sin is in their lives. Don't believe Hollywood. God has no wrath, is another lie of Satan that contradicts the Word of God.

Hollywood presents Bible believing Christians as axe murderers, insane, crazy, hypocrites, mad-men, crazy women, etc...

Some people think that Christians have no fun. That is another lie from hell. Tell me what fun a person has when they get drunk, throw up, have a splitting headache, feel awful, have a sick stomach, etc...That idea of fun, I can do without. Is it fun not to know where you were, what happened to you, why your car is dented, who you may have run over or hit while you were intoxicated, or lose your license, go to jail, be charged with crimes, etc...Satan's idea of fun is not fun.

Some people think, "When I'm old, I'll turn to God. How do you know you will be alive tomorrow? Why should you live your entire life in Satan's camp, doing his evil works, when you could have the God of Heaven, his love, joy, peace, favor, blessings, help, comfort, and Presence in your life now and forever?

Religion is the biggest demon spirit that Satan uses to keep people from knowing Jesus Christ and following Him. Religion kept the Pharisees and scribes from believing in Jesus. They died in their sins, without the Savior; because they trusted their own man-made religion to save them. Religion cannot save anyone from hell.

In John 5:39-40, Jesus said to the Pharisees and Saducees (the religious leaders) , "Search the scriptures; for in them you think you have eternal life: and they (the scriptures) testify of me, And you will not come to me, that you might have life."

In John 5:46-47 Jesus said, "For had you believed Moses, you would have believed me, for he wrote of me. But if you believe not his writings, how shall you believe my words."

Religion didn't die on a cross for you. Jesus did. Religion will never save one person from hell. There is one Savior. His Name is Jesus. Come to Him and have Everlasting Life. He Loves You. Believe on Him today.

CONTENTS
by CHAPTER

CHAPTER 1

THE DEITY OF JESUS CHRIST

When Adam and Eve sinned, sin fell on all mankind. The devil, through the serpent, tricked Eve into eating the fruit from the Tree of the Knowledge of Good and Evil. In Genesis 2:16 -17, God said to Adam, "Of every tree of the garden you may eat but of the tree of knowledge of Good and Evil, you should not eat of it. for in the day that you eat thereof, you shall surely die." Eve had not been created yet when God spoke this to Adam.

Adam told Eve they were not to eat of that tree. The devil, through the snake, questioned Eve as to what God said and put doubt into her heart. Eve said, "But of the fruit of the tree, which is in the midst of the garden, God has said. "You shall not eat of it or touch it, lest you die." The devil said, "You will not surely die." Eve ate the forbidden fruit, and gave it to Adam and he ate it also.

In Genesis 3:8 "And they heard the voice of the Lord God walking in the garden in the cool of the day: and Adam and his wife hid themselves from the presence of the Lord God among the trees of the garden." The day that they ate the fruit they died spiritually. Their close relationship with God was broken. Instead of Walking with God in the garden they hid themselves. They knew they had disobeyed him, they were naked, felt ashamed, and hid themselves. Sin always separates us from God.

God spoke to the Devil in Genesis 3:14-15 "And the Lord God said unto the serpent, Because you have done this, you are cursed above all cattle, and above every beast of the field; upon your belly shall you go, and dust shall you eat all the days of thy life: And I will put enmity between you and the woman, and between your seed and her seed; it shall bruise your head, and you shall bruise his heel." We see here that;

1

the seed of the woman would crush Satan's head. It doesn't say that the egg of the woman would crush the devil's head. It says the "seed". We know that a woman's body produces eggs, not seed. If Jesus had come from Mary's "egg", he would have had original sin attributed to him. He was never an egg. He was the Seed of the Word of God.

Romans 3:23 "For all have sinned and come short of the glory of God." Jesus is God. There was never a time when Jesus was not God. It was Jesus who walked with Adam and Eve in the garden in the cool of the day. No one can see the face of Father God and live. The Holy Spirit is in spiritual form. It was not he who walked in a physical body with them. It was Jesus Christ.

In Matthew 1:20, an angel of the Lord appeared to Joseph in a dream saying, "Fear not to take Mary for thy wife; for that which is conceived in her is of the Holy Ghost."

In Luke 1:28-35, an angel of the Lord spoke to Mary saying, in verse 30, "Fear not, Mary; for you have found favor with God, and behold you will conceive in your womb, and bring forth a Son, and shall call his name, Jesus. He shall be great, and shall be called the Son of the Highest, and the Lord God shall give unto him the throne of his father David; and he shall reign over the house of Jacob forever; and of his kingdom there shall be no end." In verse 35 the angel said, "The Holy Ghost shall come upon you, and the power of the Highest shall overshadow you: therefore, also that Holy thing which shall be born of you shall be called the Son of God". The Holy Ghost, the power of God, came upon Mary and planted Jesus Christ (Yeshua) as a seed into her womb. He is the "seed of the woman who would crush the devil's head."

Jesus is God. In John 1: 1-5, the Bible says, "In the beginning was the Word, and the Word was with God, and the Word was God. The same was in the beginning with God. All things were made by him; and without him was not anything made that was made. In him was life; and the life was the light of men. and the light shines in the darkness, and the darkness comprehended it not."

Here, we see that the Word was God. He created everything. Verse 10-13 says, "He was in the world, and the world was made by Him, and the world knew Him not. He came unto his own, and his own (most of the Jewish people) received Him not. But as many as received him, to them gave he power to become the sons of God, even to them that believe on his name. Which were born, not of blood, nor of the will of the flesh, nor of the will of man, but of God."

If we look back at the very beginning in Genesis chapter 1 verses 1-3, we see Father God, his spoken Word come forth, and the Spirit of God (the Power of God) moving and bringing everything into being. Father God spoke the Word, "Let there be light" and the Spirit of God brought forth light. We see the Father, the Word who become flesh and dwelt Among Us (Jesus), and the Holy Spirit present at creation. The entire Trinity created everything.

The prophet Isaiah prophesied in Isaiah 7:14 "Therefore the Lord himself shall give you a sign: Behold a virgin shall conceive, and bear a son, and shall call his name Immanuel (God with us)."

Isaiah 9: 6-7 "For unto us a child is born, unto us a son is given; and the government shall be upon his shoulder and his name Shall be Called, Wonderful, Counselor, the Mighty God, the Everlasting Father, the Prince of Peace. Of the increase of his government, and peace there shall be no end, upon the throne of David, and upon his kingdom to order it, and to establish it with judgement and with Justice from henceforth even forever."

These two scriptures of Isaiah speak of who Jesus is. He is Almighty God, Everlasting Father, Prince of Peace. How can Jesus (Yeshua) be listed as the Everlasting Father? Isn't there a Trinity? Yes, there is!

1 John 5:7 (KJV) "For there are three that bear record in heaven, the Father, the Word, and the Holy Ghost: and these three are one." The Word is Jesus, who became flesh and dwelt Among Us.

In John 14: 9 Jesus said, "He that has seen me, has seen the Father. I and the Father are one."

Exodus 3: 13 "And Moses said unto God, 'Behold, when I come to the children of Israel and shall say unto them, the God of your fathers has sent me unto you; and they shall say to me, "what is His name?" what shall I say unto them?'"

Verse 14-15, "And God said to Moses, "I AM that I AM: and he said, "Thus shall you say unto the children of Israel, I AM has sent me unto you."' And God said, "The Lord God of your fathers, the God of Abraham, the God of Isaac, and the God of Jacob, has sent me unto you: this is my name Forever, and this is my memorial unto all generations."

If we look at John chapter 8 verses 54-58 Jesus said, "If I honor myself, my honor is nothing; it is my Father that honors me, of whom you say, that he is your God: yet you have not known him; but I know him: and if I should say, I know him not, I should be a liar like unto you: but I know him and keep His saying. Your Father Abraham rejoiced to see my day: and he saw it and was glad.

Then the Jews said unto him, "You are not yet 50 years old, and have you seen Abraham?" Jesus said, "Before Abraham, was I Am." He was telling them that he, Jesus, always was. He was telling them that he is the I Am (the God of Abraham). In verse 59 they took up stones to cast at Jesus because he was claiming to be God.

Everywhere in the Gospel of John, Jesus kept telling them He is God; the "I Am", who appeared and spoke to Moses by the burning bush. When you think about it, God didn't limit himself to just one aspect of himself. He said, "I Am" Meaning past, present, and future. I AM, encompasses every aspect of God, not just one aspect. He is everything we need him to be – Savior, Lord, Provider, Friend, Healer, Comforter, King, our help in time of trouble, etc....

If we look at what Jesus was saying in the Gospel of John, he kept claiming to be the "I Am."

Jesus said in John 14:6 "I Am The way, the truth, and the life: no man comes to the Father, but by me."

John 15:1 "I am the true Vine."

John 10: 14 "I am the Good Shepherd."

John 6:35 "I am the bread of life: he that comes to me shall never hunger, and he that believeth on me shall never thirst."

John 10:7 "I am the door of the Sheep."

John 8:12 "I am the light of the world: he that follows me shall not walk in darkness: but shall have the light of life."

John 11:25-26 "I am the resurrection, and the life he that believes in me, though he were dead, yet shall he live. And whosoever lives and Believes In Me shall never die."

When Jesus rose Lazarus from the dead after four days, he gave his disciples an example of his ability to resurrect their bodies, also. They knew he had the power to raise them from the dead. When people understand that Jesus will give them Glorified Bodies and Eternal Life, there is no reason to fear death. II Corinthians 5:8 "To be absent in the body is to be present with Jesus."

John 5: 17-18, the Jews were angry with Jesus because He healed a man on the Sabbath. In verse 17 Jesus answered "My Father works hitherto, and I work. Therefore, the Jews sought to move to kill him, because he had not only broken the Sabbath, but said also that God was his Father, making himself equal with God."

Jesus said in John 5:39 "Search the scriptures: for in them you think you have eternal life: and they are they which testify of me, and you will not come to me, that you might have life."

In John 5: 46-47 Jesus said, "For had you believed Moses You would have believed me: for he wrote of me. But if you believe not his writings, how shall you believe my words?" Jesus Is God. He always was, is, and will be God. There was never a time when he was not.

If we look at Daniel chapter 3, King Nebuchadnezzar made a golden image, set it up, and expected everyone to worship this Idol, when music was played. Anyone who would not bow to it, would be cast into the midst of a fiery furnace. These Jews named Shadrach, Meshach, and Abednego refused to bow to this false god. In verse 17, They said, "If it be so, our God whom we serve can deliver us from the burning fiery furnace and he will deliver us out of your hand, O King. But if not, be it known unto you, O King, that we will not serve your Gods, nor worship the golden image which you have set up."

The king commanded the furnace be heated seven times hotter (in verse 19). In verses 20-22 the three Jews were bound and cast into the furnace. The men who threw them in, burned to death. And in verse 23, the Jews fell down bound into the fiery furnace.

In Daniel 3: 24-25 King Nebuchadnezzar said, "Did we cast three men, bound into the midst of the fire?" They answered and said unto the king, "True, O King." He answered and said, "I see four men loose walking in the midst of the fire, and they have no hurt; and the form of the fourth is like the Son of God."

Jesus Christ was there, in the Old Testament, walking as a man with them in the furnace, many years before he was planted into Mary's womb as a "seed", by the Holy Ghost. A full grown Jesus, as a man, was walking with Shadrach, Meshach, and Abednego, In the furnace, before He ever came forth as a baby in the manger. Jesus Is God. He always was and will be God. He protected the men, in the furnace and none of them suffered any harm at all. They were not burnt. They didn't even smell of smoke.

Beware of foolish theologians who try to explain away the supernatural miracles of God, by using their natural minds and intellect. The natural mind is an enmity against God. It denies the Supernatural. On television, I have heard the most ridiculous attempts, of theologians, to explain away the "falling of the wall of Jericho," the "fiery furnace," the" miracles of Jesus," saying he had some " special oil,"" The parting of the Red Sea," etc.... and other Supernatural, Biblical events, with their natural minds. They refuse to believe in God's ability to make the impossible, possible. Trust Holy Spirit, not them. They are so intellectually minded they are of no Heavenly good.

In Hebrews 7: 1-3 Jesus is Melchisedec described in the Scripture. It was Jesus who met Abraham returning from the slaughter of the Kings. Abraham gave a tithe to Jesus, King of Righteousness, King of Salem, King of Peace, etc.... Notice verse 3 says, "Without father, without mother, without descent, having neither beginning of days nor end of life; but made like unto the Son of God; abides a priest continually."

If we look at the times that Jesus spoke to Mary, he called her, "woman" not "mother". Jesus always was. Mary was a descendant of King David. She was the Jewish virgin, God chose to be planted in, as the "seed of the woman who would crush Satan's head." She humbled herself before God calling herself God's hand maiden. She trusted God with her life and future.

1 Timothy 3:16 "And without controversy great is the mystery of godliness: God was manifest In the flesh, justified in the spirit, seen of angels, preached unto the Gentiles, believed on in the world, received up into Glory."

1 John 3:8, "He that commits sin is of the devil; for the devil sinned from the beginning. For this purpose, the Son of God was manifested, that he might destroy the works of the devil."

John 10:10 Jesus said, "the thief comes to steal, to kill, and to destroy! I am come that they might have life: and that they might have it more abundantly."

We see here that the devil wants to destroy people. Jesus came to give them life. In John 8: 42-47 Jesus said, "If God were your father, you would love me: for I proceeded forth and came from God; neither came I of myself, but he sent me. Why do you not understand my speech? Even because you cannot hear my word. You are of your father the devil, and the lust of your father you will do. He was a murderer from the beginning, and abode not in the truth, because there is no truth in him. When he speaks a lie, he speaks of his own: for he is a liar and the father of it. And because I tell you the truth, you believe me not. He that is of God hears God's words: you therefore hear them not, because you are not of God."

We see here that Satan is a liar, a murderer, and the father of all lies. He is behind the demonic lies of– Darwinism, atheism, communism, socialism, secular humanism, Marxism, Nazism, Racism, Occultism, etc.... Evolution is a lie. Human beings are created, by Jesus, in the womb of their mother, for God's Divine Purposes. All human life is important and special. All people have a God-given right to be free, to choose good or evil, free to speak what they believe, free to hold the job they want, free to work hard and own a home, free to live and enjoy their lives without Wicked Satanic Dictators, forcing them to submit to their wicked control, fear, domination, and intimidation. We must fight against them for the sake of our children, grandchildren and future generations.

If you are a college student, realize that they refuse to let you hear conservative speech or Christian speech on campus. Why? They are brainwashing you to believe socialist / Marxist lies and don't want you to hear any truth about anything. Even in grammar schools they are indoctrinating students to hate our Constitution, our God-given freedoms, our liberties, and America.

If you are helping them to destroy our history, our monuments, our culture, our past, you are doing The Works of Hitler's Nazism. First, Hitler destroyed the history of the German people. Then, he took them over. It is demonic as hell itself.

If you are believing the CRT, demonic craziness, you are accepting one of the points of the 13 Point Communist Manifesto by Satanist Karl Marx. There is no "white privilege." Every person, I know, whether black, white, or Hispanic, that owns a house, has worked hard for years to pay a mortgage, taxes, home repairs, etc.... No one gave them anything. They worked hard and earned what they have with Blood, Sweat, & Tears. White Privilege is a satanic lie. All lies come from Satan.

> Galatians 5:1 "Stand Fast in the Liberty wherewith Christ hath made us free and be not entangled again with the Yoke of bondage."

> II Corinthians 3:17 "Now the Lord is that Spirit: and where the Spirit of the Lord is, there is Liberty." (Not Bondage)

In the beginning of this chapter on "the Deity of Christ," we established the fact that Jesus was planted into Mary's womb, by the Holy Ghost, as the "seed of the woman." Jesus would crush Satan's head. Jesus is the Word of God who dwelt among Us; Emmanuel, God With Us.

Jesus taught the parable of the Sower in Matthew 13: 3-9 and explained it further to His Disciples, in Matthew 13:18-23. When someone hears the Word of God and doesn't understand it, the Devil comes and steals the seed of the word sown in his heart. This is the seed that fell by the wayside.

He that receives the seed of the Word, the Gospel of Jesus Christ, into stony places; hears the word and with joy receives it. Yet, he has no root in himself. The word doesn't get deeply rooted in him. He follows

Jesus for a little while, but when trouble or persecution come because of the word, (his friends tease him, call him a Holy Roller, a right-wing Fanatics, a Jesus Freak), he gets offended and walks away.

He that receives the seed of the word among thorns is he that hears the word; and the cares of this world, lust of the flesh, the eye, the pride of life, mammon, the deceitfulness of riches choke the word, and he becomes unfruitful. Matthew 6: 24 you can't serve God and mammon, riches.

> 1 Timothy 6:9-10 "But they that will be rich fall into temptation and a snare and into many hurtful and foolish lusts, which drown men in destruction and perdition. For the love of money is the root of all evil. Which while some coveted after, they have erred from the faith, and pierced themselves through with many sorrows."

> Matthew 13: 23 "But he that received the seed of the word into good ground is he that hears the word, the Gospel of Jesus Christ, and understands it, which also bears fruit, and brings forth, some 100-fold, some 60 and some 30." The people who hear and understand the word, preach the Gospel of Jesus Christ. They bear the good news of the Gospel of Jesus Christ to reach other people for Jesus so that they can have eternal life also. They share their faith.

For several years my Husband Paul and I went into the Highland Residential Youth Prison, to minister to the boys. A Godly woman named June Little John was in charge of the Christian volunteers, who went into the prison. We had Tuesday night Bible studies, reached many of the boys for Jesus Christ, and helped them to see that Jesus loves them, that they and their lives were created by God and that God had a good purpose for their lives. Some got GED's and went on to college. Others joined the armed forces and others found jobs and went to work. The prison had an 85% success rate. Governor Pataki gave the prison an award. The 15% return to crime rate was probably among the boys who opted out of the Bible studies and refused God. The ones who gave their hearts and lives to Jesus had great success. Jesus changes people on the inside. They become less selfish, more caring, more loving, and more responsible and considerate of the people around them. They belong to God.

Jesus went on in Matthew 13: 24-30, To speak about the wheat and the tares. Jesus, sowed good seed – the people of God and the Word of God. While men slept, his adversary, Satan, sowed tares, lies and wicked people, among the wheat. God waited until both the wheat and the tares were grown up, to send the Reapers in. They gathered the tares, Satan's people, and burned them in the fire. God's people, the wheat, were gathered into God's Barn, heaven.

> Acts 4:10-12 "Be it known unto you all, that by the name of Jesus Christ of Nazareth, whom you crucified, who God raised from the dead, even by him does this man stand here before you whole. Neither is their salvation in any other; for there is no other name under Heaven given among men, whereby we must be saved."

Trusting in anyone else but Jesus to save you is a serious error. Only Jesus Christ can save us from hell. Philippians 2: 8 says "He humbled himself and became obedient unto death, even the death of the Cross. Wherefore Father God also has highly exalted him, given him a name which is above every name: that at the name of Jesus every knee should bow, of things in heaven, and things in Earth, and things under the Earth. And that every tongue should confess that Jesus Christ is Lord, to the glory of God the Father.

Every person, every demonic Spirit, every principality, every Power, every ruler of Darkness, every dictator, every Nazi, Marxist, communist, socialist, racist, Hollywood star, government leader, president, vice president, Congress person, Senator, judge, Governor, mayor, Dean, teacher, etc.... will bow to Jesus. Even Satan will bow to Jesus.

Once in Kisumu Kenya, Satan was stomping around my bed in the middle of the night huffing and puffing. "In the name of Jesus, I commanded him to get out of my hotel room and not return," and he left. He had to obey the name of Jesus.

Calling , "Jesus", when my car hydroplaned, Saved My Life. "For all who call upon the name of the Lord shall be saved." It is true in the natural realm as well as with the spiritual realm. Jesus is real. Jesus Is God. Jesus is Alive. He is the real God. Keep reading and you will learn so much more about Jesus, our God, our Savior, and our King. The Only Name, the devil wants to ban, in our schools, our college campuses, our businesses and in society, is the name of Jesus. Why? Because Jesus is the only way, truth and life. No one comes to God the Father, but by Jesus. No one else can save a soul, but Jesus. Turn to Him today. He loves you. He died for you. He rose again. He is Alive!

When we look at "the Revelation" we see it is the Revelation of Jesus Christ. The testimony of the word of God is the testimony of Jesus Christ. It was not the testimony of Any Other Name, but Jesus. When we study Revelation chapter 5, the only one found worthy to open the book and loose the Seven Seals was Jesus. Verse six, "and in the midst of the elders, stood a Lamb as it had been slain, having seven horns and 7 eyes which are the seven spirits of God".

> Revelation 5: 8-10 "They fell down before the lamb, having every one of them Harps and golden vials full of odors, which are the prayers of the saints. And they sang a new song, saying, "You are worthy to take the book, and to open the seals thereof: for you were slain, and have redeemed us to God by your blood out of every kindred, and tongue, and people, and nation; and have made us unto our God, Kings and Priests: and we shall reign on the Earth."

> Revelation 5:12, "Worthy is the Lamb that was slain to receive power, and riches, and wisdom, and strength, and honor, and glory, and blessing."

When we look at Revelation chapter 19:11–21, we see Jesus, the Word of God and his Heavenly armies coming from Heaven. He is the King of Kings and Lord of Lords. In verse 20, the Anti-Christ, (the Beast), and the false prophet are cast alive into the Lake of Fire, by Jesus. The armies of the Anti-Christ are slain with the sword of Jesus that proceeds out of his mouth. Jesus sends one Angel to bind Satan, the Devil, in a bottomless pit for a thousand years. An interesting fact is, that it only takes one Angel to bind up the devil. We have a great big God and an itty-bitty devil.

Revelation 22: 1-5 "And he showed me a pure River of Water of Life, clear as Crystal, proceeding out of the Throne of God and of the Lamb. In the midst of the street of it, and on either side of the river, was there the Tree of Life, which bore twelve manner of fruits, and yielded her fruit every month: and the leaves of the tree were for the healing of the Nations, and there shall be no more curse; but the Throne of God and of the Lamb shall be in it; and his servants shall serve him: And they shall see his face; and his name shall be in their foreheads. And there shall be no night there; and they need no Candle, neither light of the Sun, for the Lord God gives them light: and they shall reign forever and ever." Jesus Is God, he always was God. He will always and forever be God. His Deity is from Everlasting to Everlasting, World Without End. Amen.

1 Timothy 3:16 "And without controversy great is the mystery of godliness: God was manifest in the flesh, justified in the Spirit, seen of angels, preached unto the Gentiles, believed on in the world, received up into glory." Jesus is God. He Loves You. He died on a cross for your sins and mine so we can be forgiven and inherit eternal life in heaven. He Rose from the Dead and is the Living Lord and Savior of all who believe on 1 Believe on Him Today!

CHAPTER 2
THE BLOOD OF JESUS

People have mistaken ideas about how to get to heaven. Some believe that their works are weighed on a scale, and if their good works outweigh their bad, they can get in.

Romans 10:3-4 "For they, being ignorant of God's righteousness, and going about to establish their own righteousness, have not submitted themselves into the righteousness of God. For Christ is the end of the law for righteousness to everyone who believes."

Roman 10:9-10 "That if you shall confess with your mouth the Lord Jesus and shall believe in your heart that God has raised Him from the dead, you shall be saved. For with the heart, man believes unto righteousness; and with the mouth confession is made unto salvation."

Titus 3: 3-7 "For we ourselves also were sometimes foolish, disobedient, deceived, serving lusts and pleasures, living in malice and envy, hateful and hating one another. But after that the kindness and love of God our Savior toward men appeared, not by works of righteousness which we have done, but according to his mercy he saved us, by the washing of regeneration, and renewing of the Holy Ghost; which he shed on us abundantly through Jesus Christ Our Savior; that being justified by his grace, we should be made heirs of eternal life."

Some people believe if they are not as evil as the people around them, they will go to heaven.

In Luke 18:9-14, Jesus spoke this parable, "Two men went up into the temple to pray; the one a Pharisee, and the other a publican (publican in ancient Rome was the tax collector or a saloonkeeper or innkeeper.) The Pharisee was a "Jewish religious leader," in the temple.

The Pharisee stood and prayed like this with himself, "God, I thank you, that I am not as other men are, extortioners, unjust, adulterers, or even as this publican. I fast twice in the week, I give tithes of all that I possess. And the publican, standing afar off, would not lift up so much as his eyes unto heaven, But smote upon his breast, saying, God be merciful to me a sinner. I tell you this man went down to his house Justified rather than the other; for everyone that exalts himself shall be abased; and he that humbles himself shall be exalted."

The Pharisee thought he was better than other people, and would not repent of his own sins. He compared himself to everyone else and thought he was okay. Jesus said that the Publican was justified because he humbled himself and prayed for God to have mercy on him. He knew he was not perfect. He knew he was a sinner and needed God's forgiveness.

Some people believe that being a "good person" will get them into heaven. They do many "good deeds" trying to earn favor with God. The problem is that God's standards are so much higher than our standards that we cannot do enough "good deeds" to make up for even one sin that we have done in the sight of a holy God.

If you have ever loved someone or something more than you have loved God, you have broken the first commandment. If you have ever sworn and taken God's name in vain, you have broken the third commandment. If you have ever walked away with someone else's pen, taken a paper clip without asking, borrowed something, and not returned it, you are a thief in the sight of a Holy God. If you have ever looked at another person to lust after them, you have committed adultery with them, in your heart.

No matter how "good" we try to be, we would never be "good enough" to qualify for a place in heaven, by our own means. That is why God had to come, in human form, lead a sinless life, die for the sins of his creation to redeem fallen mankind back to himself. The sinless, Holy, Blood of God is the only sacrifice for our sins that God will accept. Jesus was and is the perfect Lamb of God who would take away the sin of the world.

The Bible says in Romans 3: 23-26, "For all have sinned, and come short of the glory of God; being justified freely by his grace through the Redemption that is in Christ Jesus. Whom God has set forth to be a propitiation Through faith in his blood, to declare his righteousness for the remission of sins that are past, through the forbearance of God; to declare, his righteousness: that he might be just and the justifier of him which believes in Jesus."

I don't know of anyone, outside of Jesus, who is sinless. As good as we try to be, we are still all sinners, in the sight of A Holy God.

Justified means, "to free from blame; declared guiltless absolve"

Redemption / redeem "To buy back, to get back, recover, to set free by paying a ransom, to deliver from sin and it's penalties, as by a sacrifice made for the sinner, to make amends or atone for"

Propitiate means "to become favorably inclined, win or regain the goodwill of."

Jesus, by his blood sacrifice for our sins, on the cross, ransomed us from the penalties of sin and death and restored us into a right relationship with Father God. Through faith in his blood, our sins are washed clean (paid for by Jesus) and we are forgiven.

Hebrews 9:22 "And almost all things are by the law purged with blood: and without the shedding of blood there is no remission."

In Genesis 3:21 we see that when Adam and Eve sinned, animals were killed to make coats for them to cover their nakedness; animal blood was shed.

In Genesis chapter 4, Abel offered to the Lord a lamb of the flock, as a sacrifice to God, a blood sacrifice. Cain offered a non-bloody sacrifice - the work of his hands, vegetables, or fruits, he had grown. God had respect for Abel's offering. Cain got jealous and murdered Abel. Abel's blood cried out to God from the ground (Genesis 4: 10). Notice here that blood has a voice and can cry out to God from the ground. Can you imagine how much innocent blood is crying out to God from abortion clinics, unmarked graves and garbage dumpsters and containers where the human remains of these babies are?

In the Old Testament, under the laws, various kinds of animals were to be brought to the outer court of the temple and sacrificed for the sins of the people. Certain birds were to be offered at a child's birth / dedication ceremony.

Once a year, only the high priest, could enter through the vail into the Holy of Holies where the Tabernacle and mercy seat were, to offer a blood sacrifice for himself and the sins of the people. He had a rope tied to his leg and bells on his Priestly robes in case he died. The bell showed the people outside that he was still moving and alive. If they didn't hear the bells for several hours, they would assume that he did something wrong and God slew him. They would use the rope attached to him to pull out his dead body. No one else could enter the holy place. The high priest was the only one who could enter with a blood sacrifice for himself and the people, once a year. No one else could have approached God, but him.

During the year, if you realized you had sinned, you would bring an unblemished, perfect animal from your flock, to offer a trespass / sin offering to God seeking his forgiveness and mercy. This offering would be done outside, by the priests, for each person who brought a sacrifice to God. The priests were busy all day long, every day, making the blood sacrifices of animals to God to atone for people's sins. If that animal blood had not been shed, the Judgment of God would have come upon the people and the blessings of God would have been withheld from the people.

> Hebrews 9: 1-4 will help to explain further. "Then the first Covenant had also ordinances of divine service, and a worldly sanctuary. For there was a Tabernacle made; the first, where in was the Candlestick, and the table, and shewbread; which is called the sanctuary. And after the second veil, the Tabernacle which is called the holiest of all; which had the golden censer and the Ark of the Covenant, overlaid roundabout with gold, wherein was the golden pot that had Manna, and Aaron's Rod that budded and the tablets of the Covenant;"

> Hebrews 9:5-15 "and over it (over the ark), the cherubim of Glory shadowing The Mercy Seat; now when these things were ordained, the priests went always into the first Tabernacle, accomplishing the service of God.

But into the second went the high priest alone once every year, not without blood, which he offered for himself, and for the errors of the people; The Holy Ghost signifying, that the way unto the holiest of all was not yet made manifest, while the first Tabernacle was yet standing; Which was a figure for the time then present, in which were offered both gifts and sacrifices, that could not make him that did the service perfect, as pertaining to conscience; Which stood only in meats and drinks, and divers washings, and carnal ordinances, imposed on them until the time of reformation.

But Christ being a high priest of good things to come, by a greater and more perfect Tabernacle, not made with hands, that is to say, not of this building; Neither by the blood of goats and calves, but by his own blood he entered in once unto the holy place, having obtained Eternal Redemption for us. For if the blood of bulls and goats and the ashes of a heifer sprinkling the unclean, sanctifies to the purifying of the flesh; How much more shall the blood of Christ, who through the eternal Spirit offered himself without spot to God, purge your conscience from dead works to serve the Living God?

And for this cause he (Jesus) is the mediator of the New Testament, that by means of death, for the Redemption of transgressions that were under the first testament, they which are called might receive the promise of Eternal inheritance."

> Hebrews 9:24-28 "For Christ has not entered into the holy Place made with hands; but into heaven itself, now to appear in the presence of God for us; Nor yet that he should offer himself often, as the high priest entered into the holy place every year with blood of others; For then must he often have suffered since the foundation of the world: but now once in the end of the world, has he appeared to put away sin by the sacrifice of himself.

And as it is appointed unto man once to die, but after this the Judgment:

So, Christ was once offered to bear the sins of many: and unto them that look for him shall he appear the second time without sin unto salvation."

Hebrews 10:12-17 "But this man after he had offered one sacrifice for sins forever, sat down on the right hand of God. From henceforth expecting until his enemies be made his footstool. For by one offering he has perfected forever them that are sanctified.

Whereof, the Holy Ghost also is a witness to us: for after that he had said before, 'This is the Covenant that I will make with them after those days, says the Lord, I will put my laws into their hearts and in their minds will I write them; And their sins and iniquities will I remember no more."

As we see from the scriptures, Jesus is no longer nailed to the cross, bleeding and dying. He is not being re-sacrificed by priests every time we take communion. He is sitting at the right side of Father God in Heaven (Hebrews 10:12). No human being has the power to pull Jesus Christ, (God the Son) out of heaven and put him into communion elements. He is God!

John Chapter 6 has been misunderstood by many churches. Here are some key verses to look at:

John 6:35 "And Jesus said unto them, I am the bread of life: he that comes to me, shall never hunger; and he that believes on me shall never thirst."

Here, Jesus is speaking of spiritual hunger and spiritual thirst. He isn't speaking about physical bread at all.

John 6:37 "All that the Father gives me shall come to me; and he that comes to me, I will in no wise cast out."

John 6: 40 "And this is the will of him that sent me (Father God), that everyone which sees the Son, and believes on him, may have everlasting life; and I will raise him up at the last day!"

Jesus mentions physical bread in John 6:49. People who ate Manna in the wilderness were dead. Eating physical bread, Wafers, matzo etc. Doesn't save anyone. Jesus Saves.

It is coming to Jesus, repenting of your sins, and believing Jesus died for your sins that saves you. Come to Jesus! Believe in the Lord Jesus Christ and you will be saved!

We saw in the description of the Holiest of All, that only the high priest could go behind the veil into the Holiest of All, near God. No one else was allowed to approach God.

> In Matthew chapter 27:50-53, "Jesus, when he had cried again with a loud voice, yielded up the ghost. (He died.) And the veil of the temple was torn in half from top to the bottom, and the earth did quake, and the rocks broke, and the graves were opened; and many bodies of the Saints (believers) which slept (had died), arose, And came out of the graves after his resurrection, and went into the holy city, and appeared unto many."

When Jesus died on the cross, the temple veil that represented sin and kept ordinary people from being able to approach God, was torn in half. The way for people to approach Father God was made open by the shedding of Jesus Christ's blood and his death for our sins on the cross.

> Hebrew 10: 19-23 "Having, therefore, Brethren boldness to enter into the holiest by the blood of Jesus, by a New and Living Way, which he has consecrated for us, through the veil, that is his flesh; And having a high priest over the house of God; let us draw near with a True Heart in full Assurance of Faith, having our hearts sprinkled from an evil conscience and our bodies washed with pure water. Let us hold fast the profession of our faith without wavering."

Through the blood of Jesus Christ, we can draw near to Father God. We can boldly enter the holy place because the Lamb of God was slain to take away our sins. We can pray to the Father, as Jesus taught us to do.

> In John 14:12-14, Jesus said, "He that believes on me, the works that I do shall he do also, and greater works than these shall he do; because I go to the Father. And whatsoever you shall ask in my name, that will I do, that the Father may be glorified in the Son. IF you shall ask anything in my name, I will do it."

Father God will hear us and answer us because Jesus Christ's blood, paid for our sins and restored us back to Father God. It is only through faith in Christ that we can be saved. Religion didn't die on a cross for you. Jesus did. Religion didn't save the Scribes and the Pharisees. Those who rejected Jesus, died in their sins. They had religion without God himself. Many people today claim to be "Christians", but they do not know Jesus Christ in their heart or life. They are not Christians because, "Christianity is Christ." They have a Godless, Christless Religion, that cannot save them from hell. Unless they repent of their sins and turn to Jesus Himself, they will lose their souls.

Jesus said in John 14:6 "I am the way, the truth, and the life: no man comes to the Father, but by me." Jesus is the only way. He alone is the Savior.

1 John 1:5-10 "God is light, and in him is no darkness at all.
If we say we have fellowship with him, and walk in darkness,
we lie, and do not have the truth: but if we walk in the light,
as he is in the light, we have fellowship one with another, and
the blood of Jesus Christ His Son cleanses us from all sin.

If we say that we have no sin, we deceive ourselves and the truth is not in us. If we confess our sins, he is faithful and just to forgive us our sins, and to cleanse us from all unrighteousness. If we say that we have not sinned, we call him a liar, and his word is not in us."

Christians are not perfect. We are just forgiven. There are some deceived preachers that have said, "Everything is all under the blood of Jesus. You don't have to repent anymore. It is all under the blood." They have even been deceived enough to say that 1 John I:1-10, is only for the unsaved people to repent and receive Jesus. It isn't for the Believers." Bologna! They are keeping the world and sin in the Church and the Christians in the world, with a license to sin, against God.

If they look at Revelation Chapter 2 and 3, the Holy Spirit is saying to the churches, "repent." The churches are told to repent! Five out of the seven churches were told by God The Holy Spirit to REPENT! If you hurt someone, you tell them you're sorry. How much more, should we tell God we are sorry, if Holy Spirit convicts us that we have sinned against Him. Should we use the grace of God as a license to sin, God forbid.

Some deceived pastors are saying that conviction and condemnation both come from the Devil. Condemnation is a work of Satan. But conviction of sin, is the work of God the Holy Spirit, to bring people to repentance and back to a close relationship with Father God, again. If you ignore Holy Spirit's conviction, and continue in unconfessed sin, eventually you will be so backslidden you won't hear God anymore. Sin separates. Repentance restores our relationship to Father God and keeps it strong. Holy Spirit's conviction is a good thing.

> John 16:7-11 Jesus said, "I tell you the truth; It is expedient for you that I go away: for if I go not away, the Comforter will not come unto you; but if I depart, I will send him unto you. And when he is come, he will reprove the world of sin, and of righteousness, and of judgment. Of sin, because they believe not on me; Of righteousness, because I go to my Father, and you see me no more; Of judgment because the prince of this world is judged." To reprove means to convict or correct. Holy Spirit reproves or corrects the believers and brings them to repentance in order that their relationship to Father God stays strong.

There are three steps to overcoming the devil, listed in Revelation 12:11. We will begin in Revelation 12 verses 7-10.

> "And there was a war in heaven: Michael and his angels fought against the Dragon (Satan); and the dragon fought and his angels and prevailed not; neither was their place found any more in heaven. And the Great Dragon was cast out, that old serpent, called the devil, and Satan, which deceived the whole world: he was cast out unto the Earth, and his angels were cast out with him. And I heard a Loud Voice saying in heaven, Now is come salvation, and strength, and the kingdom of our God, and the power of His Christ: for the accuser of our brethren is cast down, which accused them before our God, day, and night."

There are a few things here that we need to take note of. God's angels led by Michael had a battle with the dragon (Satan, the devil) and threw him and his angels Out of Heaven onto the Earth. He had accused God's people night and day.

21

Revelation 12:11 "And they overcame him (Satan) by the blood of the Lamb, and by the Word of their testimony; and they loved not their lives unto the death."

- The first thing you need to do to overcome the devil is repent of your sins and ask Jesus Christ into your heart and life. Welcome him in to be your Savior and Lord. Here is a prayer you can pray:

  Father God, I know I am a sinner. Please forgive my sins. I ask Jesus Christ, the Lamb of God, to come into my heart and life and be my Savior and my Lord. Wash my sins clean Lord Jesus, in your blood and help me to live for you. Amen.

If you have repented and asked Jesus to come in, he is now in your heart. He sees you, he hears your prayer, and if you mean it, he will save you. "For all who come to him, he will in no wise cast out."

- The second thing you need to do is to give your testimony to someone else. Tell someone that Jesus is your Savior and Lord. As you walk with Jesus, tell someone who needs Jesus, what Jesus has done for you. If you follow Jesus, the Light of Christ will shine in your heart. You will not walk in darkness but will have the light of Life. Sadly, many Christians forget that there is a third thing they need to do to overcome Satan.
- "And they loved not their lives unto the death." Let me explain with some scriptures:

  Galatians 2:20 The Disciple Paul said, "I am crucified with Christ; nevertheless, I live; yet not I, but Christ lives in me, and the life which I now live in the flesh I live by the faith of the Son of God, who loved me, and gave himself for me."

Paul was saying, "I am dead to my own plans, my own agendas, my own desires, my own will, my own purposes… I have surrendered my entire life to Jesus Christ. It is Jesus Christ Living this life, in me, to do God the Father's will, not my will. I am dead to myself and alive to Jesus. Jesus is Lord of my life, not me."

There was no part of Paul's life that wasn't surrender to Jesus. Jesus ruled and reigned in every area of Paul's life, to do Father's Will. Paul was not living a selfish, self-centered life. He was physically alive, but

Jesus was working in him to do the will of Father God. Overcoming takes trusting God, full surrender to God (Jesus) as Lord of your whole life, and accomplishing Father's Will, here on Earth as it is in heaven. Even Jesus Christ had to fully surrender to Father's Will.

> If we look at Mark 14: 35-36 "And he (Jesus) went forward a little, and fell on the ground, and prayed that, if it were possible, the hour might pass from him." "And Jesus said, Abba Father, all things are possible unto you; take away this cup (of suffering) from me: nevertheless, not what I will, but your will be done." Jesus fully surrendered to do Father's Will, not his own will.

In 1996, my Son Brian and I took a CBN tour to Israel. I had asked Jesus into my heart and life back in 1984. I had known Jesus Christ as my Savior for twelve years. While in the Church of the Nation's, near The Garden of Gethsemane, I saw a flat rock that had a rope around it, inside the church. The Holy Spirit led me to go under the rope and touch the flat rock. Immediately, I felt God's presence and was convicted by the Holy Spirit that I had been living for myself. I had never prayed and asked God to show me His will, His purpose, and His plan for my life. I had just gone on trying to please God but didn't really know what His will was. I stood there crying. I prayed, "Father God, forgive me for doing my own will. I don't even know what your will is for my life. I have never really given you my entire life." That day Kathy Hollop died, and Jesus Christ became Lord of my life. I prayed, "Father God forgive me. Lord Jesus, I surrender to you my heart, my mind, my soul, my body, my spirit, my emotions, my feelings, and my own will. I don't want my own will to be done. I want your will to be done. I give you, my life. It is now yours. Use it to your glory. Amen."

The tears were rolling down my face and God's Presence was all over me. The entire CBN group had gone outside, to the bus, and I wasn't even aware of it. I wasn't aware of anyone or anything around me, but God's presence. Brian had to come back inside, to get me.

After I surrendered my entire life fully, God began to give me dreams, guide my steps into His will, and show me what "good things" to reject and what good things lined up with His Will for me. I was led by Jesus into Father's Will and purposes.

23

The reason many people in the body of Christ, don't have victory over the devil is that they refuse to surrender their entire lives to God. Any area of your life that you hang onto is under the lordship of self and Satan. Satan has control over those areas of your life.

> Mark 8:34-35 Jesus said, "Whosoever will come after me, let him deny himself, and take up his cross, and follow me. For whosoever will save his life shall lose it; but whosoever shall lose his life for my sake and the gospels, the same shall save it." If we follow Jesus, he must be the one leading us, not ourselves. The disciples came to Jesus in Matthew 12: 46-50 and told him his mother and brothers and were outside. Jesus replied, "who is my mother? And who are my brethren? And he stretched forth his hand toward his disciples, and said, behold my mother and my brethren. For whosoever shall do the will of My Father which is in heaven, the same is my brother and sister, and mother."

When I look at the above scripture, I have to question, "who are the people who don't do the Father's Will? Are they really related to Jesus?" There is a greater glory that God wants to pour out on his people to reach lost souls and do Father's Will on planet Earth. It is described in Isaiah chapter 60.

One night (while I was in Gilgal, Kenya on a mission trip), I said, "Lord, darkness is Consuming the Earth and gross Darkness the people. Where is your Isaiah 60 Glory? Why don't you pour it out on your people?" The Lord said, "Ask my people this question, for me: "How can I trust you with my glory, if you won't trust me with your life?"

People who refuse to surrender their entire lives to Jesus, will not be able to receive the Isaiah 60 Glory. Self and Satan will cause them to misuse God's glory. Instead of doing miracles for free, they will be charging people, glorifying themselves instead of God, and puffing themselves up in pride. Only those who fully repent, receive Jesus Christ as their Savior and Lord (have their sins washed clean by the blood of Jesus), surrender their entire lives to Jesus and testify of Jesus; will be able to be entrusted with the greater glory (the Isaiah 60 Glory that God wants to pour out on the Body of Christ, His people). It requires all three things to overcome Satan.

All of the promises of God, to the churches, that are listed in Revelation Chapter two and three are to he who overcomes. There are no promises to those who give up, quit, compromise, or back slide into wickedness. Only Overcomers will inherit everything. Be an overcomer and inherit God's promises. God is true to his Word, to give the Overcomers all he has promised them.

CHAPTER 3
THE RESURRECTION OF JESUS CHRIST

In Matthew chapter 28, Mary Magdalene and the other Mary came to the tomb, where Jesus's body was lain, an earthquake happened, and an angel of the Lord descended from heaven and rolled the stone away. His countenance was like lightning, and his clothing white as snow. The angel said, "I know that you seek Jesus who was crucified. He is not here: for he has risen, as he said." The soldiers watching the tomb shook and became as dead men (with fear). Later they went into the city and told the chief priests what happened. The chief priests paid the soldiers a lot of money to lie and say, "His disciples came and stole the body, while we slept." That lie was told to keep the Jews from knowing that Jesus rose from the dead.

> Mark 16: 9-11 "Now when Jesus was risen early the First day of the week, he appeared first to Mary Magdalene, out of whom he had cast seven devils. And she went and told them that had been with him, as they mourned and wept. And they, when they had heard he was alive, and had been seen of her, believed not.

> Luke 24: 13-31 gives an account of two disciples walking to a village called Emmaus. They were speaking about Jesus's crucifixion and burial and the fact some women said they had seen angels, who said Jesus was alive. They went to the tomb and had found it empty.

If we look at Luke 24: 14-16, Jesus joined them and walked with them. It was Jesus they were speaking to. They didn't realize Jesus was standing there with them, listening to everything they were saying.

Luke 24: 25-27 "Jesus said to them, O fools and slow of heart to believe all that the prophets have spoken: ought not Christ to have suffered these things, and to enter into his glory. And beginning at Moses and all the prophets, he expounded unto them in all the scriptures the things concerning himself."

They still didn't realize Jesus was the man speaking to them. Their spiritual eyes were closed.

In verse 30 it says, "And it came to pass, as Jesus sat at meat with them, he took bread, and blessed it, and broke and gave it to them. And their eyes were opened, and they knew him; and he vanished out of their sight."

Luke 24:33-35, They returned to Jerusalem, found the eleven disciples and others gathered with them and said, "The Lord is risen indeed, and has appeared to Simon." They told what Jesus had said to them and how they knew it was Jesus, in the breaking of bread.

Luke 24: 36-39 And as they spoke, Jesus himself stood in the midst of them, and said, "peace be still."' They were terrified, fearful, and thought he was a spirit. Jesus said, "Why are you troubled? And why do thoughts arise in your hearts?"

Notice, Jesus knew their thoughts of their hearts, Jesus said, "Behold my hands and my feet, that it is I myself: handle me and see; for a spirit has not flesh and bones as you see me have." Notice, Jesus didn't say, "flesh and blood." His blood had been shed on the cross, in payment for our sins. He had no blood. Jesus showed them his hands and feet – the nail holes. They gave Jesus a piece of broiled fish and part of a honeycomb and he did eat.

In Luke 24: 44-49, Jesus said unto them, "These are the words which I spoke to you, while I was yet with you, that all things must be fulfilled, which were written in the law of Moses, and in the prophets, and in the Psalms, concerning me. Then Jesus opened their understanding that they could understand the scriptures. Jesus said, "Thus, it is written, and thus it behooved Christ to suffer, and to rise from the dead the third day. And that repentance and remission of sins should be preached in his name among all nations, beginning at Jerusalem. And you are all Witnesses of these things, and behold, I send the promise of my Father upon you, but tarry in the City of Jerusalem, until you be endued with power from on high." The promise was the Holy Ghost Baptism that happened in Acts chapter 2, on Pentecost.

In Matthew 22:23, the Sadducees, which say that there is no Resurrection, came to Jesus. They asked Jesus a question. They asked, "If a woman had been married to several men, in the resurrection, whose wife will she be"? Jesus answered them in verse 29, "You do err, not knowing the scriptures, nor the power of God, for in the resurrection; they neither marry, nor are given in marriage, but are as the angels of God in heaven". Notice it doesn't say that human beings become Angels. Angels do not marry. Neither will we, marry in heaven. We will all be "the bride of Christ" and serve him.

Even widows, here on Earth, have God as their husband. God is there for the women who have been barren, abused, ashamed, forsaken and refused. Read Isaiah 54: 1-8. "For your maker is your husband; the Lord of Hosts is his name; And your Redeemer, the Holy One of Israel; the God of the whole Earth shall He Be called." You Are Not Alone. God loves you and can restore you.

Jesus continued speaking to the Sadducees In Matthew 22: 31-32 "But as touching the resurrection of the dead, have you not read that which was spoken unto you by God, saying, "I am the God of Abraham, and the God of Isaac, and the God of Jacob? God is not the God of the dead, but of the living." They are alive.

Look at Matthew 17: 1-6 And after six days Jesus took Peter, James, and John up into a high mountain. And Jesus was transfigured before them; and his face did shine as the sun, and his clothing was white as the light. And behold, there appeared unto them Moses and Elias talking with him. In verse 4, Peter said, "Let us make three Tabernacles – one for Jesus, one for Moses, and one for Elias". Verse 5 " while Peter spoke, behold, a bright cloud overshadowed them and behold a voice out of the cloud (God the Father spoke) saying, This is my beloved Son, in whom I am well pleased; hear ye him And when the disciples heard it, they fell on their faces, and were sore afraid." There are many things we need to see in this passage.

- Moses and Elias had physically died many years before, but they were alive and standing with Jesus.
- No one spoke that it was Moses and Elias that the disciples were seeing. The Holy Spirit revealed to them, that it was Moses and Elias.
- God the Father would not permit Tabernacles of worship to be erected to Moses and Elias. He spoke and elevated His Beloved Son, over mankind, to be the One worshipped, not man.

1 Corinthians 15: 12-14 "Now if Christ be preached that he rose from the dead, how do some of you say that there is no resurrection of the dead? But if there is no resurrection of the dead, then is Christ not risen. And if Christ be not risen, then our preaching is vain, and our faith is also vain."

Verse 17 "And if Christ be not raised, your faith is vain; you are still in your sins. Then they which have died in Christ are perished." Verse 20 "But now is Christ risen from the dead and become the first fruits of them that slept. For since by man came death, by man also came the resurrection of the dead. For as in Adam all die, even so in Christ shall all be made alive. But every man in his own order; Christ the first fruits; afterward they that are Christ's at his coming." Verse 26 "The last enemy that shall be destroyed is death."

Story of Lazarus - John 11:1-41 Lazarus, the brother of Mary and Martha had physically died. He was placed in a tomb and was there four days, before Jesus arrived. In verses 33-48, we see that everyone was weeping at the tomb because Lazarus was dead. In verse 35 "Jesus wept." He felt their pain, their sorrow, their grief, and wept with them.

Martha, the sister of Lazarus said, "Lord, by this time Lazarus stinks for he has been dead four days." Verse 41 "Then they took away the stone from the tomb. Jesus lifted up his eyes, and said, Father, I thank you that you have heard me, and I know that you hear me always: but because of the people which stand by I said it, that they may believe that you have sent me. And when Jesus spoke this: he cried with a loud voice, Lazarus, come forth. And he that was dead came forth, bound hand and feet with grave clothes: and his face was bound about with a napkin. Jesus said, Lose him and let him go." Many believed on Jesus. Jesus gave his disciples and everyone there an example of what he had told them in John 11 25-26 "I am the resurrection and the life; he that believes in me, though he were dead, yet shall he live and whosoever lives and believes in me shall never die."

In raising Lazarus from the dead, in the full view of his disciples, he was showing them that if they died, he could bring them back to life. He could resurrect them also. Therefore, (after Acts chapter 2 and the Holy Spirit empowered them), they were willing to preach the Gospel of Jesus Christ, not fearing physical death. They all died violent deaths of persecution, except for John. He was in prison, boiled in oil, persecuted, but his death is not recorded. We must remember that Jesus promised eternal life to those who believe in him. They will die physically but their soul and spirit will live on, with Him in Heaven. They will receive a Glorified Body.

> 1 Corinthians 15: 41-44 "There is one glory of the sun, and another glory of the moon, and another glory of the stars: for one star differs from another star in glory. So also, is the resurrection of the dead. It is sown in corruption: it is raised in incorruption; it is sown in dishonor; it is raised in glory; it is sown in weakness; and it is raised in power; it is sown a natural body; it is raised a spiritual body. There is a natural body, and there is a spiritual body."

These scriptures are all speaking of the Resurrection from a dead natural body (a flesh body) to a spiritual body. Frankly, I'm looking forward to a body that won't need eyeglasses, won't have any knee pain or aches, never get sick, never feel tired, weak, etc.

Most of all, I am looking forward to seeing my Jesus face-to-face, meeting his disciples, meeting the Old Testament prophets, meeting relatives that I know are in heaven, seeing old friends, etc. If you really know Jesus, have him in your heart and life, read the Word and Obey him, you don't have to fear death. You know you will have eternal life in heaven, with Jesus. In speaking of "Resurrection," I must mention that there are "two "Resurrections" mentioned in Revelation chapter 20.

In Revelation 19: 20 Jesus cast the Antichrist (the Beast) and the false prophet both alive into the Lake of Fire.

In Revelation 20:4-6, The people who were murdered, beheaded, for their witness of Jesus and those who did not worship the Antichrist or his image or receive his mark in their hands or foreheads, lived and reigned with Christ a thousand years. The dead people who had served Satan were not resurrected during that thousand-year period.

Verse 6 says, "Blessed and holy is he that has part in the first resurrection on such the second death has no power, but they shall be Priests of God and of Christ and shall reign with him a thousand years."

Revelation 20:7-10 Satan is loosed to deceive the people who were born during the thousand years. They also have a choice to serve Jesus or Satan. Satan led his followers to surround the camp of God's people in Jerusalem. Fire came down from God out of heaven and devoured them. Revelation 20:10 "the devil was cast into the lake of fire and brimstone, where the Beast and the false prophet are, to be tormented day and night forever."

Revelation 20:11-15 describes a Great White Throne Judgment for those who reject the Gospel of Jesus Christ. They died in their sins and had to face the Judgment of God and his eternal punishment.

Revelation 20:12-15 "all the dead, small and great stood before God and the books (of their lives, their sins, their deeds) were opened along with the Book of Life. They were judged by God on the things written in the books." They couldn't lie, bribe God, erase his books, make excuses, or deny the things they had done. Their lives were "an open book."

"The sea gave up the dead which were in it. Death and Hell delivered up the dead which were in them. " No one, who died in their sins, escaped God's Throne judgment.

In Revelation 20:14-15, death and hell were cast onto the Lake of Fire. This is the second death. "And whosoever was not found written in the Book of Life was cast into the Lake of Fire."

The human beings who rejected Jesus Christ were cast into the Lake of Fire to be tormented day and night forever, along with Satan, the Antichrist, and the false prophet. They could have had Heaven through faith in Jesus Christ, but they chose hell and the Lake of Fire. Don't let this be you.

The last thing that Jesus said to his disciples before he ascended up into heaven is listed in Mark 16:15-18 "Go into all the world and preach the gospel to every creature. He that believes and is baptized shall be saved; but he that believes not shall be damned. And these signs shall follow them that believe; in my name shall they cast out devils; they shall speak with new tongues; They shall take up serpents; and if they drink any deadly thing, it shall not hurt them: they shall lay hands on the sick, and they shall recover." Notice that the signs listed above are for "he that believes." They are for the believers today.

We are commanded to preach the gospel, but the satanic lie of "separation of church and state," and the "ACLU" have kept Christians in America from sharing their faith. This lying law needs to be removed and the Gospel of Jesus Christ needs to be preached and shared again everywhere.

Since we are not to "tempt God" or to "put God to the test," We are not to deliberately play with poisonous snakes or drink poison. If we get bitten by a snake or we, by accident, are given the wrong prescription or a witch tries to poison us, we can stand on the scriptures.

After Jesus spoke to the disciples in Mark 16:15-18 which is "the Great Commission," He ascended to heaven. He is now Seated on the right hand of God the Father making intercession for us and waiting for his enemies to be made his footstool.

THE POWER OF JESUS'S NAME

Colossians 1:16-17 "For by Jesus were all things created, that are in heaven, and that are in Earth, visible and invisible, whether they be thrones, or dominions, or principalities, or powers, all things were created by Jesus, and for Jesus." We see here that Jesus created everything visible and invisible. He created the principalities and powers, so they are subject to him.

Ephesians 1: 17-23 pray, "That the God of our Lord Jesus Christ, the Father of Glory, may give unto you the Spirit of wisdom and revelation in the knowledge of him: The eyes of your understanding being enlightened: that you may know what is the hope of his calling, and what the riches of the glory of his inheritance in the saints, And what is the exceeding greatness of his power to us who believe, according to the working of his mighty power, Which he wrought in Christ, when he raised him from the dead, and set him at his own right hand in the Heavenly places, Far above all principality, and power, and might, and dominion, and every name that is named, not only in this world, but also in that which is to come."

We see that Father God raised Jesus from the dead, set Jesus at his own right hand, set Jesus above every principality, power and dominion and raised his name above any other name that is named. No one is greater than Jesus. Jesus is over every demonic principality, power, ruler of darkness, and Satan himself. They all must bow and submit to the name of Jesus. Even death must bow to Jesus.

In Acts chapter 3: 1 – 9 Peter and John saw a lame man (who had never walked), lying at the temple gate, begging for alms. The lame man looked at them expecting money. Peter said, "Silver and gold have I none; but such as I have, I give you; In the name of Jesus Christ of Nazareth rise up and walk. And he took him by the right hand, and immediately his feet and ankle bones received strength. And he leapt up, stood, and walked and entered with them into the temple, walking, and leaping, and praising God." People were amazed and ran toward them wondering how the lame man could walk.

In Acts 4:6-7 the high priest asked them, "By what power, or by what name, have you done this?" In Acts 4:8-12 "Peter was filled with the Holy Ghost and answered them. Peter said, Be it known unto you all, and to all the people of Israel, that by the name of Jesus Christ of Nazareth, whom you crucified, whom God raised from the dead, even by him does this man stand here before you whole. This is the stone, which was set at naught of you builders, which is become the head of the corner. Neither is salvation in any other: for there is no other name under Heaven given among men, whereby we must be saved."

Trusting in anyone else to save you, other than Jesus Christ, will lead to destruction. There is one Savior. His name is Jesus. Jesus said in John 6:37, "All that the Father gives me shall come to me, and him that comes to me, I will in no wise cast out."

Jesus said in John 6: 40, "And this is the will of him that sent me, that everyone which sees the Son, and believes on him may have everlasting life. And I will raise him up at the last day."

Philippians 2:8-11 "And being found in fashion as a man, he humbled himself, and became obedient unto death, even the death of the Cross. Wherefore God also has highly exalted him and gave him a name which is above every name. That at the name of Jesus every knee should bow, of things in heaven, and things in Earth, and things under the Earth; and that every tongue should confess that Jesus Christ is Lord, to the glory of the Father."

Even Satan must bow to the name of Jesus. I found this out in a hotel room, in Kenya. I was asleep in my hotel room. In the wee hours of the morning, I was awakened by someone stomping hard and growling around my bed. Holy Spirit said, "It is Satan." I said, "Satan, in the name of Jesus, get out of my hotel room and don't you come back, in Jesus's name." All the stomping and growling stopped immediately. I got out of bed, and turned on the light. Satan was gone. I shut the light and went back to bed. I praised and thanked the Lord for showing me that my Ministry work in Kenya, was very effective.

Satan can only be one place at a time. He is not omni-present. My God is. For Satan to be growling and stomping around my bed, I must be doing something right for God's Kingdom's advancement. Praise God!

God's Holy Spirit Power can manifest anywhere you say Jesus's name. It is not limited to Africa.

My Husband Paul and I were in the Bahamas at a Love Song Event. That day, we had attended a worship service on the beach. We went to another Island for a barbecue. Arriving back at the hotel, we sat at the poolside and ate ice cream. The Royal Towers Hotel has a huge aquarium on the bottom floor and some hallways leading outside and elevators leading back up to the rooms. As we walked through the hallway we heard and saw a crazy situation.

A man was on the floor shaking, having an epileptic fit. Two men were trying to hold him down, so he wouldn't try to stand. His wife was screaming, "Oh my God, he's going to die!" Another woman had tried to keep him from biting his tongue. She had put her hand into his mouth and was screaming, "He's biting my fingers off!" A group of Chinese people were standing a distance away watching.

First, I said, "In Jesus' name I bind the spirits of epilepsy and death. Leave this man now and don't return, in Jesus' name." Immediately the man stopped shaking. The Demonic attack was over. The woman pulled her hand out of his mouth and was amazed that her fingers were healthy and whole, not chewed, red and bitten. She kept opening and closing them in amazement, because she had felt the pain of him biting them. There were no cuts or blood on them. The man was fine, stood up, and went with his wife.

As we began walking to the elevator a young Chinese man came after us Screaming, "What did I see? What did I just see? I don't understand." I guess he was amazed that when the Name of Jesus and the authority and power of God arrived, everything changed. He wanted to know what happened. .

I said, "You have just seen the devil try to kill a man. You have seen the power in Jesus' name that has stopped the attack and healed the man. God is more powerful than Satan is." Then I gave him a "Love Story

Bible track," And said, "Jesus loves you and if you want to receive Jesus, there is a prayer on the back page you can pray. Then read the Bible. Start in the Book of John." Maybe this young man will be God's missionary to China. Only God knows the plans he has for him.

In a Ugandan Village, I saw a huge woman (she could have been a football linebacker), screaming, yelling, and waving her fists in the air. Kabaka, a Warrior Spirit was in her. She wanted to fight anyone and everyone she could. I was told that people who were oppressed by that demon would run up tree trunks, float in the air and do other demonic manifestations. I bound the demons in her that she couldn't attack me or anyone else, in Jesus' name. She couldn't come near us. Then we bound the demon and commanded it to leave her, in Jesus' name. It was stubborn and wouldn't leave at first, because she didn't want it to go away.

I have learned that if a demon / demons will not leave a person, when you speak the name of Jesus; either the person wants to keep them, or the demons have a legal right to stay.

Witches may get in prayer lines with their demonized babies or children. They hope to occupy all of the pastor's, missionaries, or evangelist's prayer time with their children, so that the rest of the people, in the prayer line won't be ministered to.

No one can cast those demons out of the children, If the parents who have the spiritual authority over them, want the demons there. Sometimes the parents have made deals with witch doctors. In one case, the parents sold their child to the witch doctor for a field of sugarcane. The girl who was around twelve years old, was running outside, taking off her clothes, rolling in the mud, making strange sounds, etc.... demonized.

I prayed for the girl and commanded the demons to leave her, in Jesus' name. They wouldn't go. That night, the Lord revealed to me that her parents had traded her to the witch doctor for the sugarcane fields they had. Unless they repented (they claimed to be Christian) and returned the sugarcane field, their child could not be delivered. They made a demonic deal with Satan.

One day, my car was hydroplaning into the oncoming lane. A huge, food store delivery truck was coming at me. I tried to turn the wheel to get my car back into the right lane, but I couldn't do it. I screamed, "Jesus!", closed my eyes, gripped the wheel, and waited for the impact. It never came. When I opened my eyes, the truck was in my rearview mirror. My car was back on the right side of the road, and I didn't do it. My Jesus did.

"For all who call upon the name of the Lord shall be saved." This scripture also holds true in the natural Realm.

A Venezuelan Pastor went to the bank in Venezuela. Four men jumped him, hit him over the head and robbed him. One of the men spoke of pulling him into the car, driving away and murdering him. The Pastor said, "Jesus." Immediately the men jumped into the car and drove away. The demons in them had to flee when Jesus was mentioned. The pastor was stitched up at the hospital and is still alive.

Once in Mombasa, Kenya, the violent drunk (who beat up half the town), charged at me during an open-air meeting. I pointed my finger at him (the finger next to my thumb), and said, "Jesus." The man hung his head, turned, and walked away. Five Muslim men had heard me preach about Jesus. They said, "She wasn't afraid of him, Her God must be the real God," and they accepted Jesus as their Savior and Lord. They joined the local church and are helping pastors to reach more Muslims for Jesus.

Thieves in Uganda were putting something in people's house cooling units to make it hard to breathe. The people would open their doors and the thieves would rob them. Most properties had huge fences, gates and heavy chains and locks surrounding them, the houses, and the people inside. I was staying in a pastor's house. During the middle of the night, I heard people at his gate, trying to cut through the locks and chains. I said, "In Jesus name, I bind the demons in the people at the gate who are trying to come onto this property. You go away now, in Jesus' name." Immediately the rattling of the gate chains stopped. They went away and didn't return, at least while I was there.

I have heard stories involving Christians who were victims of demonized people. If they had only bound the demons in Jesus' name, or spoken the name of Jesus, they would have been saved.

If I am ever on an airplane and terrorists try to take it, I will say, "I bind every demon in these terrorists that they cannot harm or kill anyone on this plane or on the ground, in Jesus' name". Once they are bound in Jesus' name, they cannot do anything. Every Power is subject to Jesus. Jesus is the name above every name ever named. Every demon must bow to Jesus. Satan must bow to Jesus. Jesus' name is powerful. He is God!

Matthew 16:18-19 Jesus said, "I will build my church; and the gates of hell shall not prevail against it. And I will give unto you the keys of the kingdom of heaven: and whatsoever you shall bind on earth shall be bound in heaven and whatsoever you shall loose on earth shall be loosed in heaven." Jesus gave this ability to His People, the body of Christ. WE can bind the demons in people that they cannot manifest against us, In Jesus Name.

While doing a crusade in a village, in Uganda, a woman came up to me. She showed me a small bag and said the witch doctor had placed it on her door. He told her that if she removed it, she would go crazy. He terrorized the villagers with witchcraft. I said, "You will not go crazy, in Jesus' name. Give me the bag". During the Crusades, I preached that Jesus is the real God and he had more power than anyone else. I threw the Witchcraft bag and its contents on the Crusade platform dumped gasoline on it and burnt it up. I continued to preach the Cross of Christ, the blood of Jesus to save sinners etc.... when I gave an altar call, many came to Faith in Jesus. The witch doctor was angry.

The next day, the witchdoctor planned to attack me while I was on the platform preaching. Pastors saw him trying to climb up and grabbed him. They wrestled him to the ground and a huge knife fell out of his clothes. He got away from them and ran around the side of the Crusade platform to the front. I pointed my finger at him and said, "In the name of Jesus you will not come on this Crusade property again." With that, several people, he had been terrorizing, kicked him off the property and received Jesus as their Savior. That was on a Wednesday. I stayed there doing Crusades and Bible teachings several more days. The witch doctor never came back.

While in Tanzania, the pastor's, interpreters, Jane (a woman who made audio tapes of the meetings), and I, had to stay in a horrible Hotel. There was nowhere else we could have stayed. Drugs, alcohol, prostitution, and all kinds of things were going on. Jane and I shared a room. The Bible says, having done all, we stand. Because the door had only a hook latch on it, I realized Jane and I were not safe. I barricaded the door all the way across the room to the wall, using both twin beds, luggage, and anything else I could find. I did all I could do to keep us safe. In the wee hours of the morning, I heard three men outside my window talking. "Mzungu," meaning, "white person." I was the only white person in Tarime, Tanzania.

I whispered, "In Jesus' name, I bind the demons in these men outside my window. They cannot attack us or enter this room, in Jesus Name." With that, they went away. The demons, in them, had to obey the name of Jesus. Demons can hear you bind them, even if you whisper, are in another town, another country, etc.... they hear you when you speak "Jesus."

> Luke 10: 17-19 "And the Seventy returned with joy, saying, "Lord, even the devils are subject unto us through your name." And Jesus said unto them "I saw Satan as lightning fall from Heaven: Behold, I give unto you power to tread on serpents and scorpions, and over all the power of the enemy: and nothing shall by any means hurt you." (KJV)

Jesus is speaking of power over the demonic spirits (serpents and scorpions, snakes and spiders). Some Bibles have mistakenly changed the word power to "Authority". Authority with no power is useless. This is why I preach only from the King James Bible.

While at Pastor Ungundi's Church in Butere, Kenya, A boy who died came back to life by the Holy Spirit's Power and the Name of Jesus. The boy, who had been suffering with malaria for two weeks, was dying. His mother, in Faith, believed that if she could get him to the church, he would be healed. She carried her five-year-old son, in her arms, and walked many kilometers to the church.

I had been preaching on Job 22 on "the power of decrees." The pastor, his wife and I were having tea after the service, in a side room. We heard a horrible wailing, "My boy is dead! He is dead!" As we ran outside, the Holy Spirit filled me. I pointed my finger at the dead boy and said, " I command you spirit of death and malaria to leave this boy now, in Jesus Name. In Jesus Name, you will live. You will fulfill on your days on planet Earth, and they will not be shortened, in Jesus' name." The dead boy's eyes opened, he sat up and was alive, healthy, and whole, in Jesus' name. Even death must listen to Jesus.

If God's people could realize the authority, we have in Jesus' name and the spiritual power we have available to us, through the Holy Spirit, we could take the whole world, back for Christ. Jesus Is God. Satan is just a fallen angel.

These are just some things the Lord has used me to do. He wants to use you to do these things and even greater things if you let him use you. Everything that he has made available to me, is available to All His People. Press into Jesus. Read the Bible. Believe his 8,800 promises that are yours, through faith in Christ.

Fight the good fight of Faith. Be a soldier in God's Army. Stand for Christ and don't compromise. Don't throw in the towel or quit. Walk in the Holy Spirit Power. If God is with us, who can be against us. No weapon formed against us will prosper, in Jesus' name. Amen.

CHAPTER 4

BE SEXUALLY PURE WHICH IS RIGHT IN GOD'S SIGHT

Romans 12:1 "Present your bodies a Living Sacrifice, holy, acceptable unto God, which is your reasonable service."

Matthew 19: 4-6 "And Jesus answered the Pharisees who asked him, " Is it lawful for a man to put away his wife for every cause?" Jesus said, " Have you not read that he which made them at the beginning made them male and female, and he said for this cause shall a man leave father and mother, and shall cleave to his wife: and they two shall be one flesh? They are no more two, but one flesh. What therefore God has joined together, let not man put asunder.'"

When two people engage in intercourse, they become one. They join their bodies, their souls, minds, and their spirits together. Their souls which involve their emotions, their feelings, their free will... are joined to that other person. Their spirit's ability, to love deeply, is joined to that other person unless the connection is broken by the blood of Jesus.

This joining and becoming one was supposed to be within a marriage between a man, born a man, and a woman, born a woman. It was supposed to be a permanent relationship- a marriage to each other, for their entire life, on planet earth until death parts them. They were to be fruitful, bear children, and raise them up to know God. They were to teach them to understand the eternal truths of the Word of God and to have the mind of Christ. They were to be walking in truth, righteousness, kindness, goodness, love, peace, joy, and all the blessings of God and fruit of the Holy Spirit.

When two people join by having sex, they leave a part of themselves with every person they have sex with, and they take pieces of their sexual partners with them. They are joined physically, mentally, emotionally, and spiritually with the other person / persons because they have become one flesh.

We are not just physical beings. We are souls and spirits housed in physical bodies. Each person is a trinity. We have a physical body, a soul (mind area) and a spirit (heart area). When God made people, he created us in his own image. He is a trinity, Father, Jesus, and Holy Spirit. He is one God in three persons.

There are many Trinity examples in nature. Time, distance, and matter is one example. An egg is made up of a white part, a yolk, and a shell. So, an egg white, a shell, and a yolk, equal one egg. God the Father, the Son Jesus, and the Holy Spirit, equal one God.

> 1 Corinthians 6:13-20, " Now the body is not for fornication (sex outside of marriage), but for the Lord; and the Lord for the body. And God has both raised up the Lord and will also raise us up by His own power.

Don't you know that your bodies are the members of Christ? Shall I then take the members of Christ, and make them the members of a harlot? God forbid.

Don't you know that he which is joined to a harlot is one body? For two, he said, shall be one flesh. But he that is joined unto the Lord is one spirit. Flee fornication. Every sin that a man does is without the body; but he that commits fornication sins against his own body.

Don't you know that your body is the Temple of the Holy Ghost; which is in you, which you have of God, and you are not your own? For you are bought with a price; (the blood of Jesus), therefore glorify God in your body, and in your spirit, which are God's."

As a Christian, we are to love God enough to put all sexual sin out of our lives permanently. We are to Value the people we meet and not exploit them, take advantage of them, use them, or lure them into sexual sin against God.

> 1 Corinthians 7:9 "But if they cannot contain; let them marry. For it is better to marry than to burn."

Revelation 22 :14-15 "Blessed are they that do his Commandments, that they may have the right to the tree of life and may enter in through the gates into the city. For (outside the gates) are dogs, and sorcerers, and whoremongers, and murderers, and idolators, and whosoever loves and makes Lies." These locked outside, are the worldly Christians who would not put the sexual sin and dabbling in the occult, idol worship, etc. out of their lives. They are the foolish Virgins locked out forever, in Matthew Chapter 25:1-13.

"For if you live after the flesh, you shall die; but if you through the Spirit, (Holy Spirit), do mortify the deeds of the body, you shall live."

Galatians 5:24 "They that are Christ's have crucified the flesh with the affections and lusts. If we live in the Spirit (Holy Spirit), let us also walk in the Spirit (Holy Spirit)."

Years ago, when I was growing up, there were only a few girls, in my high school, that were having sex with boys. All the boys went after them, asked them out, and wanted to see what they could get from them, because they were "easy." The rest of the girls studied hard, went to church, obeyed their parents, and waited for marriage to have sex. Most of them, in my generation, are still married to the same spouse.

Now, anyone who doesn't "put out," lose their virginity, fornicate, sleep around etc.... is made fun of, ridiculed, and mocked by their peers, and Hollywood. It is a different world – but certainly not a better world.

This world has perverted Biblical marriage, convinced people that they can be both male and female, (other than who God created them to be,), and promoted lust, fornication, perversion, adultery, the deliberate ruination of the Innocence of children, sex trafficking of children, the rape of children, pornography in the school libraries, etc... It is a Filthy, Wicked World!

When I was growing up, we didn't have to worry about whether we were pregnant. We weren't having sex with anyone outside of marriage. We didn't have to worry about catching AIDS, VD, gonorrhea, and other venereal diseases from sleeping around.

There are many benefits to sexual abstinence and purity. We didn't have to sneak out, sneak around, feel guilty, hide anything, etc.... We were able to enjoy our youth, our carefree moments, our childhoods, without facing adult problems before we were ready to face them. Children's minds, hearts and bodies were protected from immorality, lust, filth, perversion... They went to Sunday school, learned about God, heard the Bible stories, were taught that it was wrong to steal, lie, falsely accuse others... They grew up strong, healthy in body, soul, and spirit, protected, loved, nurtured, valued... They grew up knowing that if they studied hard, worked hard, tried hard, they would succeed in life. They grew up knowing that God created them for His Divine Purpose, and He had a good plan for their life. They knew they were loved by Jesus the God of Heaven and their lives were valuable. They worked summer jobs at age 16. They didn't lazily sit around all summer, doing nothing. They worked to buy their school clothes, school supplies, and shoes. Parents didn't have much in material goods, but they gave us love, values, protection, and security. They were there for us. We had curfews, guidelines, instruction. If we disobeyed, we were punished. They loved us enough to correct us, direct us, guide us, teach us right from wrong according to God's Word, give us values, morals, kindness, the ability to give love and receive love (not lust and filth), but brotherly/sisterly love – caring about other people- helping others - unselfish, genuine love, honesty, decency, truth, values... We need to get back to these aspects of life.

When we look at sexual sin and the two being one, we realize that many people are not whole in body, soul, and spirit. When you become one with another person,, any demons (demonic activity), in the other person are implanted inside of your body, soul, and spirit. You are joined to them permanently unless you repent of your sins, receive Jesus Christ as your Savior, and Lord, and break the psychological ties, soul ties, spiritual ties, emotional ties, and physical ties to the people you have had sex with, by pleading the blood of Jesus Christ, to sever it all.

If you are a victim of rape, molestation, or incest, you can be set free of all of it, healed of all of it, and restored from all of it. It does not have to control your present or your future.

A Christian girl, who is very close to our family, was raped by a man who stood up in church and told how Jesus Christ changed his life. He was a wolf in sheep's clothing pretending to be Christian. He took her out on a date, raped her and then vanished from her life. She was hurt, deeply wounded, and angry at God. She couldn't understand why a "Christian man" would rape her. She couldn't understand how God could let that happen to her.

Unfortunately, God gave people free will. Many people use their free will to do wickedness, instead of righteousness. They choose to follow Satan, worldly lusts, and selfish wickedness instead of God and Truth. The girl was an innocent victim of a crime done against her by a man who lied, deceived everyone, and claimed to be someone he wasn't. Because he raped her, there were physical ties, soul ties, and spiritual ties, that needed to be broken off of her life. Her whole personality changed. It was obvious to her parents that she was angry with God, but they didn't know why. The devil told her, "You are not a virgin anymore. No decent man will ever want you." Then Satan placed an evil man into her life, convinced her to run away from her parents and take off. Her parents loved her and tried to get her to stay home, but she left. Her parents wondered if the man had gotten her on drugs. They searched her room and found the diary that recorded the account of the rape that happened to her a year before.

Because her parents were Christian, they sought the Lord Jesus Christ as to what to do to help their daughter. The Lord said, "Rip out the diary pages that are in her handwriting of the account of the rape that happened to her and burn them off of your property." In obedience, the mother brought a small metal bucket, put the pages into it, and burned them on the roadway, off the property. Once that was done, the mother prayed, and said, "In the name of Jesus Christ, I break all soul ties, spiritual ties, and physical ties between my daughter and this man who raped her, off of her life now and off of her future, in Jesus' name." Amen.

Mark 16: 17 (KJV) Jesus said, "In my name they shall cast out devils." Real Christians who have Jesus Christ as their Savior and Lord, have the power to cast out devils, in Jesus' name.

The mother said "In the name of Jesus, I command all demons, demonic activity, and anything that entered her by this rape, null, void and of no effect. It will not rob her present, her future, and God's plan for her life, in Jesus' name."

The mother also prayed that her daughter would see the wicked man, she had run off with, for who he really was. She prayed, "Bind up my daughter's womb. Don't let her have a baby by this crazy man. Bring the man you have for her into her life. Break off the physical, soul, and spiritual ties to the man who raped her, and to the man she is with now, in Jesus' name. Amen!"

It took some months, but the Lord answered the mother's prayers. The daughter realized the man was cheating on her, was violent, was on drugs, and was abusive. She ran away from him to an apartment where some friends were. The man came after her and her friends had to phone the police. By the time she came home, she was dating a nice man who was God's choice for her. She has been happily married to the nice man, has three children, and a decent life. God restored to her what Satan tried to rob from her. God can restore your life also, if you are willing to repent of your sins, ask Jesus to be your Savior and Lord, and break the spiritual, soul, and physical ties to anyone who has molested or sexually abused you, used you, or that you willingly gave yourself to, by the Blood of Jesus Christ.

To be completely free, you must forgive anyone who sexually abused you, broken your heart, used you and deserted you etc.... When you ask God to help you forgive, he will remove the unforgiveness from your heart and restore your life. He will heal your wounds, make you a whole person, and enable you to continue, in the present, and have a good future. Refuse Satan's plan to destroy your life. Jesus is able to save, deliver, and heal you; if you want him to and ask him to.

For anyone caught in the demonic web of pedophilia, there is help for you. When a child or person is raped, the demonic spirits, in the rapist, enter the person's body, soul, and spirit, wounding them deeply. They may hate the person or persons who have done these things to them, but as they get older, they find that they, themselves, are sexually abusing their own children, or other people's children. They may hate what they are doing but have no power to stop it. They are demon driven to do what they hate and don't want to do. If you are willing to be free, Jesus Christ can and will deliver you.

The following steps will help you to be saved, forgiven, delivered from pedophilia, and healed from what was done to you.

1. John 3:16 – 21 "For God so loved the world, that he gave his only begotten son (Jesus), that whosoever believes in Him should not perish, but have everlasting life. For God did not send his son into the world to condemn the world: but that

the world through him might be saved. He that believes on him, (Jesus), is not condemned: but he that doesn't believe, is condemned already, because he has not believed in the name of the only begotten Son of God. And this is the condemnation that light is come into the world, and men loved darkness rather than the light, because their deeds were evil. For everyone who does evil hates the light (they hate Jesus), neither will they come to the light, lest his deeds should be reproved (corrected). But he that does truth comes to the light (Jesus), that his deeds may be made manifest, that they are wrought in God."

Jesus came and died on the cross for your sins and mine so we could be forgiven and have eternal life. He rose from the dead on the third day. He is the living Savior and Lord of all who repent of their sins and believe on him.

Jesus said, in John Chapter 6:37, "All that the Father gives me shall come to me; and him who comes to me, I will in no wise cast out." If you repent of your sins, ask God's forgiveness, and ask Jesus Christ to come into your heart and life and be your Savior and Lord, he will come in. You will have God's Holy Spirit dwelling in you, with Christ's Authority, and God's power. John 14:16-17 The Holy Spirit will dwell with you and shall be in you.

1. You must ask Father God to help you to forgive anyone who raped, molested, used, or abused you. By forgiving them, you are letting go of the past, of the emotional pain, soul ties, spiritual pain, and memories of those incidents that wounded you. If you want Father God to forgive your sins you must be willing to forgive others, in obedience to God.

2. Matthew 6:14-15 "For if you forgive men their trespasses, your Heavenly Father will also forgive you: but if you don't forgive men their trespasses, neither will your Father forgive your trespasses." No one will get into heaven with unforgiveness in their heart.

3. Matthew 18: 21-35 Peter asked Jesus, "How often shall my brother sin against me, and I forgive him? Till seven times? Jesus said, I say not unto you until seven times: but, until seventy times seven." We cannot harbor any unforgiveness toward anyone. We must forgive.

47

4. Jesus went on to tell a parable in Matthew 18: 23 – 35 about a king who forgave a servant a great debt. But the servant refused to forgive another servant of a smaller debt. In verse 34-35 "And his Lord was angry and delivered the one who refused to forgive to the tormentors, so he should pay all that was due unto him. So likewise, shall my Heavenly Father do unto you, if you from your hearts don't forgive everyone his brother their trespasses." The tormentors are demonic spirits that keep the past, the memories, the hurt, the pain, the misery, fresh in the person's mind, heart, and spirit, year after year after year. That is why a person who was hurt 20 years ago, remembers that incident like it happened today. They have not been willing to forgive the person / persons that wronged them. They are victims of the past and are still victims, in the present, and in the future, if they refuse to obey God and forgive.

5. Forgiving someone sets you free of the memories, the hurt, the emotional pain, the spiritual wounds, and enables you to start anew. By refusing to let go of hatred, unforgiveness, and bitterness, you open the door to the tormentors, demonic activity in your life, and are in rebellion against God who says You must forgive. If you love your unforgiveness more than you love God, your unforgiveness has become your God.

6. Forgiving someone does not keep them from being accountable to God, for what they have done to you. It is an act of getting your heart, mind, and spirit healed and free to follow God, with the rest of your life. Once you forgive and let go, God can move in your life and deal with the person/persons who wronged you. Once you repent and ask Jesus to be your Savior and Lord, pray and ask the Holy Spirit to bring to your mind the names and faces of anyone you have not really forgiven. Only the Holy Spirit of God can reveal to you what is locked up in your own heart.

7. When I prayed and asked the Holy Spirit to show me anyone I hadn't really forgiven, I was shocked to discover that I had not really forgiven anyone. He brought to my memory the names and faces of people I hadn't thought of in

years. A girl, back in grammar school, who made fun of my Boston accent, came to my mind. Another girl in junior high that threatened to beat me up, came to mind. My own sister my own mother, several other relatives and ex-friends came to mind. As the Holy Spirit showed me, I said "Father God, I repent for holding onto unforgiveness against this person. I release it to you. I pray for them that they will be saved, in Jesus' Name. Amen." Person by person I forgave, let go of my unforgiveness, and prayed for their salvation, in Jesus' name. Amen. At the end of it all, I felt free, unhindered in my walk with Jesus, cleansed from the past and able to minister to other people who needed to forgive.

No unforgiveness is worth holding onto. No unforgiveness, hate, bitterness, and resentment are worth missing heaven for. Let it go today. Let God heal you of the past and move on.

8. Once you let go of the hate, unforgiveness, and bitterness pray, "Father God, I obeyed you and forgave. Now, in the name of Jesus, I cast the tormentors, the memories of the past, and all demonic activity including any spirits of lust, sexual sin, sexual perversion, fornication, adultery, pornography, gayness, homosexuality, bisexuality, transgender, and pedophilia, out of my life. Get out now and never return, in Jesus' name, Amen! I disconnect myself from all physical, emotional, soul, and spiritual ties to these people who have wronged me, in Jesus' name. Amen! I take back any pieces of myself they have taken from me and give back to them any pieces of themselves that they left in me, in Jesus' Name. Amen! Now, in Jesus' name, I am whole in body soul and spirit. Amen."

It is very important that if you have been divorced, you forgive your ex-spouse. If you harbor hate, unforgiveness, and bitterness against them, you are disobeying God and you are open to demonic spirits and tormentors. The hurt, pain, heartbreak, etc.... is locked up inside of you and will destroy your present and your future. You must forgive. You need to pray and ask the Lord, by the blood of Jesus, to sever any physical, emotional, and soul ties to your ex, in Jesus' name. You also need to say, "In the name of Jesus, I give back to my ex-spouse everything that belongs to them, and I take back from them everything that belongs to me so I can be whole, in Jesus' name. Amen!"

Unless you do these things, you are destined to fail in any future marriage because you are dragging your ex-spouse, their shortcomings, the negative feelings, emotional pain, heartbreak, resentment, hatred, your wounds, your brokenness, etc.... Into a new marriage. The new spouse suffers because they are married to a broken, wounded, hateful person who takes it out on them for something someone else did to them. You must forgive whoever has wronged you, broken your heart, cheated on you, betrayed you, wounded you, hurt you etc.... Otherwise, you will stay a victim of the past and continue the cycle of hate by wounding and hurting the other people around you. They will then spread the hatred to others.

You can never be free, or healed until you forgive, let it go, and get rid of it. Once you forgive, God will remove it and the tormentors from your life. He will remove the pain, hurt, memories, anguish, etc. and give you his love, his peace, his joy, and a fresh beginning.

> Luke 4: 18-19, Jesus read Isaiah 61: 1-2, "The Spirit of the Lord is upon me, because he has anointed me to preach the gospel to the poor, he has sent me to heal the brokenhearted, to preach deliverance to the captives, and recovering of sight to the blind, to set at Liberty, them that are bruised, to preach the acceptable year of the Lord." Jesus closed the book.

> In Luke 4:21 Jesus said, "This day this scripture is fulfilled in your ears." Jesus can set us free, heal us, deliver us from demons and tormentors, open our eyes to the truth, heal our bruises, heal broken hearts, and lives, and restore us completely.

SATAN IS A LIAR A PERVERTER OF THE TRUTH

Satan is a liar and the "father of lies." The lie that a girl can be a boy and a boy can be a girl is totally against God and God's Will and purpose for their lives.

Fact – a girl can cut her hair, take male hormones, tattoo her body, lift weights, dress like a boy, but she will never be a "real boy" or a "real man." She will never grow a penis. She will never have sperm to impregnate anyone. The transgender drugs, she takes, will destroy her female organs and her ability to conceive and birth children. Any future generations, of people, that would have come into existence, through her, are all cut off and will never be. She will spend her life trying to be someone she can never really be. Her DNA and hormones will always show that she is a female. There is no way her DNA or chromosomes will be changed to male ones.

Fact – a boy can dress like a girl, talk like a girl, act like a girl, have breast implants, but he will never grow a uterus, and ovaries, or be able to give birth to children. He will always be a "pretend girl" or a "pretend woman." the female transgender drugs will destroy his ability to produce sperm or father a child. His DNA and chromosomes will always show he is a male. There is no way to change the DNA or chromosomes to the opposite gender.

These young people were created in their mothers' wombs, by almighty God. God makes no mistakes, Satan wants to deceive and destroy the youth of our nation physically, sexually, spiritually, and emotionally. This lie of transgender, many genders, multiple genders, changing genders at one's whim etc.... is all contrary to Nature, contrary to God's Will, contrary to who they really are, and openly wrong in the sight of God. It is all "population control", designed to destroy the reproductive organs of our youth.

Parents, see if there are "transgender books and other pornographic books in your children's School library. Many public-school teachers have been convincing small children to change their genders, without their parents' knowledge. They are deliberately confusing your children sexually, robbing their innocence, exposing them to lustful, wicked cartoons, pictures, filth, and perversion. This must be stopped now.

The teachers who have refused to follow these wicked curriculums are being fired. It is time that parents demand the wicked perverted, teachers, school boards, superintendent's, curriculum producers, be prosecuted. There are still laws against showing children pornographic pictures, cartoons, images, etc.… These things are all in the transgender books and other perverse books in the school libraries. We must rid our schools of all the demonic lusts, perversions, and filth that they want to destroy our children with. We must vote against anyone who is calling parents terrorists because they care about what their children are being taught in school.

Once a child sees pornographic books, cartoons, and sexual images, you cannot erase it from their minds. Once they are brainwashed into believing they can be a girl one day and a boy the next day, they are totally confused. "Why should your children be forced to call a " girl", he, and a" boy", she , or be disciplined by the teacher?"

Why should a boy who "feels like a girl"be able to compete in the girls' sports and steal their scholarships? It is not right. Why should a boy be able to say, "I feel like a girl today," and invade the privacy of the girl's locker room, bathroom, shower stalls, etc. Why can't teachers try to stop this craziness, without losing their jobs?" The ones promoting this craziness should be fired, along with the superintendents of the schools, the wicked school boards, and the people who produce their perverted, pornographic and lustful curriculums. They should be prosecuted and jailed for giving children pornographic materials. There are still laws against giving pornography to children. They should be enforced in our schools and public libraries. Why should people who hate God and live lifestyles of rebellion against God be able to teach our children to rebel against God?

Romans chapter 1:21-32 " Because that, when they knew God, they glorified him not as God, neither were thankful; but become vain in their imaginations, and their foolish heart was darkened. Professing themselves to be wise, they become fools, and changed the glory of the Incorruptible God unto an image made like to corruptible man, and to birds, and four footed beasts and creeping things, wherefore God gave them up to uncleanness through the lusts of their own hearts, to dishonor their own bodies between themselves: Who changed the truth of God into a lie, and worshipped and served the creature more than the Creator, who is blessed forever. Amen!

For this cause God gave them up unto vile affections for even their women did change the natural use into that which is against nature; and likewise, also the men, leaving the natural use of the woman, burned in their lust one toward another; men with men working that which is unseemly, and receiving in themselves that recompense of their error which was meet.

And even as they did not like to retain God in their knowledge, God gave them over to a reprobate mind, to do those things which are not convenient. Being filled with all unrighteousness, fornication, wickedness, covetousness, maliciousness, full of envy, murder, debate, deceit, malignity, whispers, backbiters, haters of God, despiteful, proud, boasters, inventors of evil things, disobedient to parents.

Without understanding, without natural affection, implacable, unmerciful: Who knowing the Judgment of God, that they which commit such things are worth of death, not only do the same, but have pleasure in them that do them."

Do we want our children to believe that gayness is an alternative lifestyle? Do we want our children to be told it is all right to be gay, against the Word of God? Do we want our children to have" reprobate minds"? Do we want them to be like Sodom and Gomorrah, and be judged by God and destroyed? Even the children of Sodom and Gomorrah were full of ungodly lust, perversions, and reprobate minds. They were destroyed by God along with their wicked parents.

Jude verses 7-8 "Even as Sodom and Gomorrah and the cities about them in like manner, giving themselves over to fornication, and going after strange flesh, are set forth for an example, suffering the Vengeance of Eternal fire."

In Genesis Chapter 18: 20-21 "And the Lord said, because the Cry of Sodom and Gomorrah is great, and because their sin is every Grievous: I will go down now and see whether they have done all together according to the cry of it, which is come unto me; and if not, I will know."

In Genesis chapter 19: 1 - 28, two angels of God entered Sodom. Lot brought them into his house and fed them. The men of the city surrounded Lot's house. Verse 5 "And they called unto Lot, and said unto him, Where are the men who came into you this night? Bring them out unto us that we may know them." They wanted to have sex with them. Verse 7, Lot said, "I pray you, Brethren, do not so wickedly." Verse 11 The Angels smote the men with blindness, but the men kept trying to find the door to get at the angels to have sex with them. Verse 24 Then the Lord rained upon Sodom and Gomorrah brimstone of fire from the Lord out of heaven. And he overthrew the cities." This will be your fate if you refuse to repent and seek God. Gayness is Wickedness in the sight of Almighty God.

If you are or have been involved in the sin of gayness, fornication, adultery, sex with beasts, pornography, sex trafficking, pedophilia, you can repent, receive Jesus into your heart and life, and be delivered from these things. There are spirits behind all of this, promoting their ungodly lusts. They can be cast out and broken off your life if you want to be delivered from them. Some of these things are generational curses that need to be broken off your family trees. Some is a result of sexual abuse you may have suffered, and it is manifesting through you now, to attack others.

The devil will rise people up to call me a " hater", because I love you enough to tell you the truth in the hope you will repent, receive Jesus and be set free from ungodly lusts. A real hater condones your sin, accepts it, says it's okay, and doesn't care whether you go to hell for all eternity, or not. God loves you and wants you to get right with him. The choice is yours to make. Ask the Lord to lead you to a born-again, Holy Spirit-filled church with a Deliverance team who can cast the demons out of you and set you free from Satan's grasp. You can be free. Those who, the Son of God, (Jesus Christ), sets free, are free indeed.

CHAPTER 5

BE RENEWED IN THE SPIRIT OF YOUR MIND

Romans 12:2 "And be not conformed to this world: but be transformed by the renewing of your mind, that you may prove what is that good, and acceptable, and perfect will of God."

When a person repents of their sins and asks Jesus Christ to come into their heart and life and be their Savior and Lord; the Holy Spirit of God enters, and bears witness with their spirit that they are a child of God and a joint heir with Christ. You can find this in Romans 8: 8-17. This is the beginning of your relationship / friendship with Almighty God through faith in the Blood of Jesus Christ.

You still must be delivered from the worldly ideas, ideologies, lies, deceptions, fears, wrong thought patterns, sinful mindsets, sinful lifestyles, etc.... by Renewing Your Mind with the Bible – God's Word of Truth. If you don't read the Bible and renew your mind, you will continue in the lies, deceptions, mindsets, ideologies, of the devil – the enemy of all mankind. He operates in lies because he is the father of lies and abides not in the truth.

Jesus confronted demonic people in John 8: 43-47. Jesus said, "Why don't you understand my speech? Even because you cannot hear my word. You are of your father the devil, and the lusts of your father you will do. He was a murderer from the beginning, and abode not in the truth because there is no truth in him. When he speaks a lie, he speaks of his own: for he is a liar and the father of lies. And because I tell you the truth, you don't believe me. He that is of God hears God's words. You hear them not, because you are not of God."

There are many people, on planet earth, who resist God's word, God's truth, God's light, God's wisdom, God's instruction, and God's Direction and purpose for their lives. They call anyone who tries to tell them the truth, a "hater," "Holy Roller," a "religious nut", a "fanatic," or a "Jesus Freak." Being called names makes me rejoice.

> In Matthew 5:11-12, Jesus said, "Blessed are you, when men shall revile you, and persecute you, and say all manner of evil against you falsely, for my sake. Rejoice and be glad for great is your reward in heaven; for so they persecuted the prophets, which were before you." If I am called names, my reward in heaven will be greater. Praise God!

Did it ever occur to these "name callers" that these "right-wing fanatics" may be living right in the sight of Almighty God? Their lives may be filled with God's love, peace, Joy, gentleness, kindness, and goodness. They may be blessed in their family life, their finances, their health and in every way possible.

Usually, if you look at the "name callers," they walk in hatred – not love, bitterness not happiness, broken lives, destroyed marriages, and much destruction and misery that the devil has inflicted upon them.

Instead of God's truth, they believe the lies of the media, television, Hollywood, social media, Darwinism, Marxism, Socialism, New Age, Communism, Evolution/Atheism, Nazism, racism, CRT, secular humanism, woks, cancel Culture, BLM, KKK, cultural Marxism, Planned Parenthood, transgender, soap operas, etc....

The satanic lies and Liars are trying to destroy America, Christianity, values, morals, truth, love, righteousness, kindness, Integrity, the real history of America, our Christian Roots, our faith in Christ, God's Holy Bible, our freedoms, our liberties, our God-given Constitution, and " we the people." They want to subject us to the murderous tyranny of the ism's - communism, socialism, Marxism, racism, secular humanism, Darwinism, atheism, Nazism and every other form of demonic fear, control, manipulation, and wicked brainwashing.

Ephesians 4:28 "Let him that stole steal no more: but rather let him labor, working with his hands the thing, which is good, that he may have to give him that is in need." Wicked politicians want to do away with our laws against stealing and any punishment for criminals. They want to allow thieves to break into our businesses and steal the merchandise that the business owners have had to pay for. This ungodly, wicked lawlessness must stop now. Otherwise, no one will start a business, be able to hire workers, prosper from their hard work, or be able to continue in business and live peaceful lives.

The wicked, lawless politicians want to decrease our police forces and promote all kinds of lawlessness, destruction, murder, rape, and violence in our cities and towns. They do not care about " We the People," at all. They want to destroy our freedoms, our liberties, and our nation, and subject us to Wicked government control, tyranny, and slavery under Karl Marx's communism and socialism. They, the "so-called elitists," Plan to make us all slaves to them, their will, their wicked desires, their control, their brainwashing, their mandates and restrictions, their decrees, their demonic ideologies, and their Satanism.

Communism, Socialism, and Marxism are all Satanic ideologies that steal people's freedoms, God-given talents and abilities, liberties, truth, justice, righteousness, love, morality, decency, peace, Joy, etc.... They murder anyone who protests against them, once they take control of a nation. Look at Communist China.

The college students in Beijing China had a peaceful protest against their government, in Tiananmen Square. The demonic, communist government shot them down as dogs. Communists have no regard for human life. They are Satanists.

The Cubans recently wanted freedom from their wicked government. They protested. The Cuban Army was trained by communists to imprison, torture, and murder anyone who opposed them.

Personally, I know what goes on in Cuba. Back in 1973, I worked for a company as a key punch operator. One of the other key punch operators was a woman from Cuba, under Castro. Her relatives published a paper against the tyrant Fidel Castro. They were put in prison, tortured, and murdered by him. She had to flee Cuba for her life. Anyone related to the family or family friends were subject to prison, torture, and death.

Communists murder their opponents quickly. Under communism and socialism, everyone gets the same low pay, and they are deliberately kept in dire poverty, by a wicked, demonic, controlling government of murderous criminals, at the top. No one can own a home, a business, or prosper if they work hard. The lazy, slothful, people get the same pay, as hard workers, so why work hard? You can't change jobs. The government controls your job. You can't have more than one child. The government keeps track of your menstrual cycle and forces you to have Abortions whether you want them or not. The government puts you in government owned apartments. If you object to the government's control of you and your life, they can throw you out on the street with nowhere to live. Or they can pull you out of your bed, in the middle of the night, take you outside, and execute you.

Wake up America, stop Communism now! Darwinism, Marxism, Communism, Socialism, BLM, CRT, leads to horrible genocide and death tolls all over the world.

There is no love, no mercy, and no tolerance shown to anyone who opposes the wicked slavery of communism, socialism, and Marxism. They imprison torture and murder anyone who dares to confront oppose or stand up to this demonic system of slavery. Anyone desiring to worship Jesus Christ freely, or owns a Bible, is on their hit list along with anyone who wants freedom, liberty, truth, righteousness, values, morals, honesty, and justice. Christians living in communist countries must hide their worship, hide their Bibles, hide their beliefs, hide their faith in the real God of Heaven; or the fake god of government will destroy them. In China, many Christians have been imprisoned, their mouths were filled with gravel, and they were beaten to death by the demonic Chinese government, recently. This happens now.

To pretend that China is for God, they allow government controlled, "so-called churches", to operate. They control what is preached and what cannot be preached. As wicked people in the south made up a "slave bible" and took out the freedom scriptures, these wicked communists alter the truth of the Word of God and refuse to allow the entire Bible to be preached.

The real house churches of God are still being persecuted in China by the wicked, satanic, communist government. The government imprisons, tortures, and murders groups of people who will not worship it, instead of God. The Chinese government is even stealing people's organs after murdering them and doing organ transplants. Every wicked, demonic, satanic thing is being done to innocent people by the tyrants of communism, Socialism, and Marxism. They have destroyed millions of people all over the globe. Their target now is America.

Wake up! Stop them! Put an end to this now . The racism, the woks, the cancel culture, the CRT, BLM, KKK, destroying our history, destroying our police forces, burning our cities, destroying businesses and free enterprises, indoctrinating our children with satanic lies, closing our churches, stealing our freedoms, stopping truth from being taught or shared, agenda 21, dividing our nation and groups to fight each other, (while they step in and take over us) is all part of the 13 points of communism.

> Matthew 12:25 "Every Kingdom divided against itself is brought to desolation; and every city or house divided against itself shall not stand."

Americans must stand together against the slavery of Darwinism, Marxism, Communism, Socialism, racism, woks, BLM, CRT and every other ism. If we let these wicked people divide us by black versus white, young versus old, vaccinated versus unvaccinated, etc... while we are fighting each other, the communist/socialists will steal our nation.

One of the points in Karl Mark's 13 points of communism is to divide people using the media to stir up hatred, bitterness, unforgiveness, etc....To take over a nation.

Karl Marx was a Satanist. He came up with the satanic government control ideologies of communism/Socialism/BLM, CRT (part of Marxism) to destroy Christianity, enslave people, rob their ambition, their God – given freedom, liberties, abilities, talents, and their very lives. Yes, everyone would be "equally poor" and have nothing they could call their own. The government would rob you of self-will and force you to conform to its will or die.

Very few people realize that Hitler was an evolutionist who believed in Darwinism. He believed only one race of people would survive. He wanted it to be his race, so he murdered millions of innocent people. Evolution is an anti-God, anti-Christ religious theory of atheism. It denies that God created everything seen and unseen, by His power and might. It denies the entire Bible and raises up generations of people who know not God.

It is Not A Science. It is the Religion of Atheism-the belief that humans evolved from apes and that there is no God. It attacks the beginning of the Bible that says, "In the beginning God created the heaven and the earth." It teaches children the lie that there is no God and no Divine purpose and plan for their lives. They are "just evolved apes." Their lives are by chance and they have no real reason or purpose for being alive. If you view yourself as an ape, What is your life worth? If you view everyone as an evolved ape, what is the reason for their existence? It is easy to rape, steal from, and murder someone, if you view them as just an evolved monkey. If you view yourself and others as special, unique creations of Almighty God, your life and the lives of others are valuable. God Created Everyone and Everything. Children need to be taught the truth.

People who don't read the Bible have been deceived by the atheist "Religious theory of evolution." It is not a science. It is man's attempt to explain how he came to exist, without believing in a Divine Creator – Almighty God.

> 1 Timothy 6:20, (KJV), "Oh Timothy, keep that which is committed to your trust, avoiding profane and vain babblings, and oppositions of science falsely so-called: Which Some professing have erred concerning the faith. "

You cannot be a real Christian and embrace the lie of evolution, which denies Christ. You can't serve God and Satan and his lies. "No, lie is of the truth." There is no such thing as a "superior race."

> In Revelation 7: 9–17, there is a multitude of people of every nation, kindred, and tongue, standing in heaven before the thrones of Father God and the Lamb Jesus Christ.

> In verse 14 it says"These are they which came out of great tribulation and have washed their robes and made them white in the Blood of the Lamb."They are believers in Jesus Christ from every ethnic background (every race), Every tongue, every nation… God is not a racist. Neither should we be racist. God loves all the people he created in the wombs of their mothers. Everyone who repents of sin and believes Jesus died for them on the cross and rose again, is accepted by God. He created them all. He loves them all.

1 Corinthians 10:20–22 "But I say that the things which the Gentiles sacrifice, they sacrifice to devils, you cannot drink the cup of the Lord, and the cup of the devils; you cannot be partakers of the Lord's table, and of the table of devils. Do we provoke the Lord to jealousy? Are we stronger than he?"

Many Christians, "so-called", are trying to walk a tightrope. They are half in God's kingdom and half in Satan's kingdom. Let me give you some examples:

A woman, in a church choir, put on a "good Christian Act" for everyone to see. She was going to bars, prostituting herself for money, drinking, drugging... When demons would attack her, she would phone me hysterically screaming, "pray these demons off me! "She would repent and turn back to Jesus, for a short time, and then waltz with the devil again. She was playing games with God and using his grace as a license to sin. She didn't love Jesus enough to depart from evil. She loved her sin more than she loved the Savior.

Finally, I said to her, "By your wicked works, you are disgracing the name of Jesus. You are claiming to be a "Christian "when you are serving Satan and not God. If you go back and do this wickedness again, don't you call my house. I will not be used by you as a crutch to condone your sin. Where do you think you will go if you keep this up? Do you really think that you will get into heaven? Fear God and depart from evil. Stop it now, in Jesus' name, stop it!"

Titus chapter 1: 15–16 "unto the pure all things are pure. But unto them that are defiled, and unbelieving is nothing pure; but even their mind and conscience is defiled. They profess that they know God; but in works they deny him, being abominable, and disobedient, and unto every good work reprobate. "This scripture makes it clear that people who claim to know God can be defiled in their mind and in their consciences.

If you don't read the Bible, study the scriptures, believe the Word of God, obey the Holy Spirit when he shows you that you are doing wrong, you are probably as deceived and backslidden as the woman that sang in the choir. The devil is out there as a roaring lion, seeking who he can devour. His target is Christian's. He already has everyone else in his pocket. If he can tempt a Christian into sin, to destroy their church, their marriage, their family, their witness, their health etc.… He will do it.

Hollywood, the media, wicked television programs, secular magazines, tabloids, Internet sites, etc.… Can easily be used by Satan to deceive people, stir up wrong emotions, fill people with hate, lust, bitterness, lies, etc.… God's Word says "fornication "sex outside of marriage is a sin.

The world's lie is, "everyone is doing it. "If you don't do it, you are "a square, "a nerd, a freak, weird, etc.… Young people are being indoctrinated into being "lovers "by Hollywood, not realizing it is destructive sexual sin and lust in the sight of Almighty God.

God calls it "fornication. "Soap operas promote "adultery "and make people believe the lie that "everyone is doing it, it is glamorous, the grass is greener on the other side, you are missing out on something wonderful, "etc.… It is the cause of many divorces, broken lives, broken hearts, broken children, hurt, pain and misery. That is why God says, "Thou shall not commit adultery. " God tries to spare people from the destruction that ungodly lusts will do to them and their families.

If Christians would read and study God's word, they would know that Harry Potter is an abominations to God and would not allow their children to watch and read wizard books and have them in their homes. Pokémon in Hebrew means "there is no god. "Yet, Christians let their children watch it, have Pokémon cards, figures, etc.… Ouija boards, dungeons and dragons games, tarot cards, witchcraft books, spellcasting, enchantments, Deuteronomy chapter 18: 9–12 list all kinds of a cult practices that are abomination to God. The people that do these things are making themselves an abomination unto the Lord. I discuss these things in another chapter in more detail. You cannot serve God and Satan. Joshua 24:14 "now fear the Lord and serve him in sincerity and in truth: and put away the gods which your fathers served on the other side of the flood, and in Egypt: and serve the Lord. "

Joshua 24:15 "as for me and my house, we will serve the lord. "The Bible says that Jesus is the bride groom. He is coming back for his bride – his people who love him. If you were a bride groom, would you want a bride who only loved you a little but loved many other men as well? If you were a bride, would you want a groom who loved you, but had many other women he also loved? Why would Jesus take a bride who is lukewarm, rebellious, disobedient, and worships other gods beside him?

In John 14:23 Jesus said, "If a man loves me, he will keep my words: and my Father will love him; and we will come unto him and make our abode with him." If you don't read the Bible, how can you know what Jesus has said? How can you keep his words if you don't know what they are? Jesus went on to say, "he that loves me not, keeps not my sayings: and the word which you hear are not mine, but the Father's who sent me."

THE LOVE OF MONEY IS THE ROOT OF ALL EVIL

I Timothy 6:10-12 "But they that will be rich fall into temptation and a snare, and into many foolish and hurtful lusts, which drowned man in destruction and perdition. For the love of money is the root of all evil: which while some covered after, they have erred from the faith, and pierced themselves through with many sorrows. But you, Oh Man of God, flee these things; and follow after righteousness, godliness, faith, love, patience, meekness fight the good fight of faith, lay hold on eternal life."

When our lives are over, we will take nothing with us. All our earthly possessions will be left behind. We can't take our money, our houses, our cars, our awards, our trophies, our college degrees, etc.... With us.

Every day we should thank God we have a place to live, clothes on our back, food in our bellies, indoor plumbing, electricity, freshwater to drink, our family, friends, and for our very lives.

Psalm 49:6–10 "They that trust in their wealth and boast themselves In the multitude of their riches; none of them can by any means redeem his brother, nor give to God a ransom for him: (For the redemption of their soul is precious, and it ceases forever.)"

You cannot buy your salvation. You can not use wealth and riches to buy a place in heaven for yourself or anyone else. You cannot pay God a ransom (a bribe) for their soul. Your money and riches are useless things, when it comes to eternal life in heaven. Only those who believe in the Lord Jesus Christ will be saved. "For all who call upon the name of the Lord Jesus Christ Shall be saved."

Frankly, I would rather be content with what I have, and know Jesus as my Savior and Lord, then have all the riches, fame, and fortune the devil gives people to steal their souls. When you have Jesus, you have everything you need. If you reject Him, you have nothing.

> 1 John 5:9–13 "If we receive the witness of men, the witness of God is greater: for this is the witness of God which he has testified of his Son. He that believes on the Son of God has the witness in himself: he that believes not God has made him a liar; because he believes not the record that God gave of his Son. And this is the record, that God has given to us eternal life, and this life is in his Son. He that has the Son has life; and he that has not the Son of God has not life, These things I have written unto you that believe on the name of the Son of God (Jesus); That you may know that you have eternal life, and that you may Believe on the name of the Son of God."

People who have Jesus Christ, have heaven and eternal life to look forward to. People who reject Jesus will have eternal death and damnation. Those who have the Son of God have life those who reject the Son of God are liars in the side of God because they refuse to believe the witness of Father God, concerning Jesus Christ the Son of God. It is vital that people repent of their sins and believe on the Lord Jesus Christ to be saved. There is no other way to heaven. There is no other sacrifice for sin, acceptable to Father God, but the blood of His Son Jesus, shed on the cross for your sins and mine. Jesus is the lamb of God who paid for the sins of the world.

> John 14:6 Jesus said, "I am the way, the truth, and the life; no man comes to the Father but by me. "He is the only way, truth, and life. Jesus is not a Greek myth, a vain philosophy, a fable, etc.… He is the creator of everything seen and unseen.

Read the Gospel of John. Pray and ask the Holy Spirit to help you to see who Jesus really is. Get to know Jesus in your heart, soul, and mind. Let the truth of God 's words come in and permeate you with eternal truths that never change. God 's truth is truth for all eternity; now and forever. His truth never changes. He is the same yesterday, today, and forever. What God says is right, will always be right. What God says is wicked and wrong, will always be wicked and wrong. What God says is sin will always be sin in his sight. Man may try to condone things that God says are evil, but God has not changed his mind. Eternal truths never change. God doesn't change. Many may try to make excuses for sin, but God hates sin and accepts no excuses for it.

Many may think God doesn't see what they are doing. But God is Omnipresent – He is everywhere. God is Omniscient – He sees and knows it all. God is Omnipotent – He is All Powerful and Almighty. Nothing is hidden from God's sight. Everything is written in heavens books. See Revelation 20:11-12.

No person, especially in America, can say they didn't have a Bible to read. The problem is that 80% of people who claim to be Christian, never read their Bibles. They spend hours on Facebook, game sites, fantasy games, watching television, going on chat rooms, reading magazines, romance novels, etc.... And no time reading God's Eternal book – the Bible. They have Bibles, in their homes, on shelves, collecting dust, while the devil defeats and destroys them because they don't have God's truth in their minds and hearts, where it matters. How can you obey the Word of God, if you don't read and know what God says about anything? How can you raise up your children to follow and obey God, if you aren't following and obeying God yourself?

Colossians 3:16 "Let the word of Christ dwell in you richly in all wisdom; teaching and admonishing one another in Psalms and hymns and spiritual songs, singing with grace in your hearts to the Lord. And whatsoever you do in word or deed, do all in the name of the Lord Jesus, giving thanks to God the Father by him.

Psalm 119: 105 "Your Word is a lamp unto my feet, and a light unto my path. "Psalm 112:1 "Blessed is the man that fears the lord, that delights greatly in his commandments. His seed shall be mighty upon earth: the generation of the righteous shall be blessed. Wealth and riches shall be in his house: and his righteousness endures forever. "

There is nothing new under the sun. The same Temptations and trials of life happened to the people generations before we were born. The Bible uses them, their issues, their problems, their strengths, their weaknesses, to speak to us today, If we Read the Bible. Life's lessons, God's help, God's truth, God's promises are all there in his Holy Bible. The Bible gives us wisdom, Understanding, counsel, direction, and instruction from God, who truly knows everything. He and his Word are the best guidance for a happy, healthy marriage, proper discipline of children, how to overcome the devil, how to fight the good fight of faith, how to have victory in our situations, etc...

Without reading the solid word of God, you are like a ship tossed to and fro by every lie, deception, half-truth, and craziness the devil, the press and Hollywood, and wok , etc.... have to offer you. There are over 8,800 promises that God has given to believers in Christ. If you don't read the Bible, you won't know what they are, how to access them and how to apply them to your life. God 's people are being destroyed for lack of knowledge of his Word. Read the Word and grow in your faith. Become the devil 's worst nightmare as you quote scripture into every situation. The Word of God is our sword. Know it. Speak it against the devil and watch him flee from you. God is true to his word to perform it. Walk in victory not defeat, in Jesus's Name. Amen

Ephesians 6:11-13 "Put on the whole armor of God, that you may be able to stand against the wiles of the devil. For we wrestle not against flesh and blood but against principalities, against powers, against the rulers of darkness of this world, against spiritual wickedness in high places.

Wherefore take unto you the whole armor of God, that you may be able to withstand in the evil day, and having done all, to stand. Stand therefore, having your loins girt about with truth," (God's Word is Truth). Read God's Holy Bible and stand with God's Truth and not Satan's lies.

> Ephesians 6:14B and having on the breastplate of righteousness (know that through faith in Jesus, we have Christ's Righteousness attributed to us). Man's righteousness if filthy rags. We have God's Righteousness.

> Ephesians 6:15 "And your feet shod with the preparation of the gospel of peace." Be ready to share your faith in Christ wherever you go. Blessed are the feet of them that bring the good news.

Ephesians 6:16 Above all, taking the shield of faith , wherewith you shall be able to quench all the fiery darts of the wicked." No matter what is happening in your life, don't get angry with God, don't backslide, don't give up and quit, and don't let the devil rob your faith. Ask Father God to give you more faith. Ask Him for Greater Faith to believe that He is working out everything to your good. Ask Him for the gift of faith to believe for the impossible to be possible. He will never leave you nor forsake you. The Lord will carry you through to the other side. He will enable to get you through this, if you rely on Him, lean on Him and trust Him.

Ephesians 6:17 "And take the helmet of Salvation." The helmet of salvation is worn on your head to protect your mind and thoughts from the enemy. It is up to you to refuse any thought that doesn't line up with the Word of God. Every wicked deed a person does, begins as a thought. If you continue to allow yourself to think wrong thoughts, you open a door to the devil. Eventually you will do what you keep thinking about. Covetousness, greed, lust, stealing, lying, adultery, fornication, every sin begins in the mind first and then results in actions. There is a saying, "You can't stop a bird from flying over your head, but you can stop it from nesting in your hair.

You can't stop the enemy from giving you a wrong thought, but you can refuse it and cast it out, in Jesus Name.

There are many traps the devil has set for people. Watching soap operas is one of them. A woman may think, "I wish my husband was as handsome, as smart, as nice, as considerate, dressed as nice, bought me presents, like that man does" A man may think, "I wish my wife would lose some weight, dress in nice clothes, treat me like that woman treats him" etc...Reading steamy romance novels is another trap. Why don't I feel like she does? Why doesn't my husband satisfy me like he does her? I must be missing out on something. Watch Out! Satan wants to destroy your marriage and your life. Avoid lustful music. Watch out!

Renew your mind with God's Words. Philippians 4:8 "Finally,

brethren, whatsoever things are true, whatsoever things are honest, whatsoever things are just, whatsoever things are pure, whatsoever things are lovely, whatsoever things are of good report; if there be any virtue, and if there be any praise, think on these things.

> Ephesians 6:17 "and the Sword of the Spirit, which is the Word of God; praying always with all prayer and supplication in the Spirit; and watching with all perseverance and supplication for all saints"

Here we see that our Sword is the Word of God. If we don't read and know the Word of God, we won't have a sword to swing at the devil. People who don't read God's Word have a small jack knife against the devil.

> Hebrews 4:12 "For the Word of God is quick, and powerful, and sharper than any two edged sword, piercing even to the dividing asunder of soul and spirit, and of the joints and marrow, and is a discerner of the thoughts and intents of the heart."

Memorize key verses of the Bible that will help you to stand in faith. One of my favorite verses is Luke 10:19. Jesus said to Believers, "Behold I give unto you power to tread on serpents and scorpions, and over all the power of the enemy and nothing shall by any means hurt you." I have power over all the power of Satan, my enemy. Jesus gave it to me. Know all the wonderful gifts He has given to you. Read the Word of God.

CHAPTER 6
WHO IS THE HOLY SPIRIT?

John 14: 15-17, "If you love me, keep my commandments, and I will ask the Father, and he will give you another Comforter, that he may abide with you forever, even the Spirit of Truth, whom the world can not receive because it sees him not, neither knows him, But You know him, for he dwells with you and shall be in you".

John 14:26 "But the Comforter, which is the Holy Ghost, whom the Father will send in My name, he shall teach you all things, and bring all things to your remembrance, whatsoever I have said unto you." We see in the scriptures that God the Father gives to His people another Comforter, the Spirit of Truth, the Holy Ghost who teaches us the Word of God.

If we look at Romans 8:8-10

"So then they that are in the flesh cannot please God. But you are not in the flesh, but in the Spirit, if so be that the Spirit of God dwells in you. Now if any man have not the Spirit of Christ, he is none of his. And if Christ be in you, the body is dead because of sin; but the Spirit is life because of righteousness." Notice here the Spirit of God (the Father) and the Spirit of Christ is the same Spirit. He is the Holy Spirit. If any man does not have the Holy Spirit, he doesn't belong to Christ. There are many theologians, church pastors, church ministers, elders, deacons, and lay people who claim to be Christians that do not have the Holy Spirit of Father and Jesus. They do not really belong to God. They are none of his.

The Bible goes on to say In Romans 8:11, "But if the Spirit of him that raised up Jesus from the dead dwell in you, he that raised up Christ from the dead shall also quicken your mortal bodies by his Spirit that dwelleth in you."

> Romans 8:14-17, "For as many as are led by the Spirit of God, they are the sons of God for you have not received the spirit of bondage again to fear; but you have received the Spirit of adoption, whereby we cry, Abba, Father".

Without the Holy Spirit, a person is not a real child of God. They are not connected to Jesus or to the Father and are outside of God's will, plan, and purpose for their life. That's why Jesus told Nicodemus in John 3:1-5 " Except a man be born again he cannot see the kingdom of God." Nicodemus asked Jesus how he could enter his mother's womb and come out again. In John 3:5, Jesus replied, " Except a man be born of water and of the Spirit he cannot enter the kingdom of God. That which is born of the flesh, is flesh, and that which is born of the Spirit is Spirit, you must be born again."

There is a physical birth (a flesh birth), when we come out of the womb, but we must be born of the Holy Spirit of God to belong to God. When a person repents of their sins, believes Jesus died on the cross for them, And asks Jesus to come into their heart and to be their Savior and Lord, Jesus comes in. The Holy Spirit of Father and Jesus Comes into their heart and they are born again into God's spiritual family. Their name is written in Jesus's Book of Life. They are not just flesh, they are spiritually born.

> 2 Corinthians 1: 20-22 "For all the promises of God in Christ are yes and in him Amen, unto the glory of God by us. Now he which established us with you in Christ, and anointed us, is God; Who has also sealed us, and given the earnest of the Spirit in our hearts."

> Ephesians 1: 12-13 "That we should be to the praise of his glory, who first trusted in Christ. In whom you also trusted, after that, you heard the word of truth, the gospel of your salvation: in whom also after that you believed, you were sealed with that Holy Spirit of promise,"

Notice, They were sealed by the Holy Spirit after they believed the gospel and trusted in Christ. Before that, religion, their works, good deeds, their own ways, etc... did not seal them with the Holy Spirit. It was full faith in Christ that got them sealed, born of the Holy Spirit and adopted unto God's spiritual family. Without the Holy Spirit, they were not a child of God. They did not have God the Father, Jesus Christ, or The Inheritance and Promises of God through Christ. They did not have a spiritual rebirth (born- again) experience. All they had was the flesh birth, vain religion, and their own righteousness which God says is filthy rags.

> John 16: 7-11, Jesus says, " It is expedient for you that I go away: for if I go not away, the Comforter will not come unto you; but if I depart, I will send him unto you. And when he comes, he will reprove the world of sin, and of righteousness, and of judgment: Of sin, because they believe not on me; Of righteousness, because I go to my Father, and you see me no more; Of judgment, because the prince of this world is judged." Some deceived preachers have attributed the conviction (reproof\correction) of the Holy Spirit to the devil. Conviction is the Holy Spirit's work. He shows people their sin, brings them to repentance and keeps their relationship with the Father right, true, and pure. A Christian who refuses to repent, when the Holy Spirit shows them they have sinned, is like the foolish virgins in Matthew 25. They will not be ready when Jesus returns.

They will add sin to sin until their conscience is seared as in Titus 1:15-16 "Unto the pure all things are (pure); but unto them that are defiled and unbelieving is nothing pure; but even their mind and conscience is defiled. They profess to know God; but in their works they deny him, being abominable and disobedient and unto every good work (reprobate)."

These false preachers have even gone so far as to say that 1John Chapter1 is only for the unbelievers to come to Christ. When we deny that the Bible is for everyone, and we think we can pick and choose what we want and throw the rest away, we are on very dangerous ground.

When the Conviction of the Holy Spirit is attributed to Satan, blaspheme of the Holy Spirit takes place. In Mark 3:22-29, Jesus spoke of the Blaspheme of the Holy Spirit right after the scribes accused Jesus of casting out devils by Beelzebub. Jesus cast out devils with Holy Spirit's Power.

Both my husband and I have heard deceived preachers say that "Conviction and Condemnation" both come from the devil. They say foolish things like, "It's All Under the Blood of Jesus. We don't have to repent anymore."

If a Christian refuses to obey the Holy Spirit and repent of the sin that He convicts them of, they stay in their sin and get farther and farther away from Father God and His will and purpose for their life. Over time, they become more rebellious, stubborn and disobedient. They grieve the Holy Spirit by their pride and disobedience and refusal to obey Him. After a while, He will leave them to their own devices. Should we use the Grace of God as a license to sin? God Forbid.

If you have sinned, repent. Ask God's forgiveness. Humble yourself and tell God you are sorry. Then put the sin out of your life. Go and sin no more. The message to some of the churches from the Holy Spirit in Revelation Chapters 2 and 3 is "Repent or else".

John 16:13-15 "When he, the Spirit of Truth is come, he will guide you into all truth; for he shall not speak of himself; but whatsoever he shall hear, that shall he speak; and he will show you things to come. He shall glorify me for he shall receive of mine, and shall show it unto you. All things that the Father has are mine, and He shall show it unto you."

The Spirit will guide us into all Truth.

The Spirit hears what the Father and Jesus are saying and speaks it to us.

The Spirit can show us things to come.

The Spirit glorifies Jesus.

The Spirit reveals to us the Will of Father God and Jesus, for our lives.

The Holy Spirit wrote the Bible. Yes, He used many writers but they wrote what He, God the Holy Spiritt, directed them to write.

2 Peter 1:19-21 "We have a more sure word of prophecy, whereunto you do well to take heed, as unto a light that shines in a dark place, until the day dawn, and the day star arise in your hearts; Knowing this first, that no prophecy of scripture is of any private interpretation. For the prophecy came not by the will of man: but <u>holy men of God spoke as they were moved by the Holy Ghost.</u>"

How did King David in Psalm 22, generations before Christ came, know what Christ would suffer, but by the Holy Ghost.

How did the Prophet Isaiah know every detail about Jesus's death on the cross for our sins in Isaiah 53, many generations before Jesus came to earth? Isaiah wrote about the rejection, the persecution, the wounds, bruises, pain, for our transgressions and our iniquities. He wrote about people going astray and the Lord laying upon Jesus the iniquity of us all. Isaiah wrote about Jesus's silence, hanging between two thieves, being placed in a rich man's tomb, etc.... The Holy Spirit revealed the future about what the Christ would suffer, to the prophet Isaiah.

The Holy Spirit told them these things would happen generations before they happened.

1 Corinthians 2:9-14 "But as it is written, Eye has not seen, nor ear heard, neither has entered into the heart of man, the things which God has prepared for them that love him. But God has revealed them unto us by his Spirit: for the Spirit searches all things, yes, the deep things of God. Now we have received, not the spirit of the world, but the spirit which is of God: that we might know the things that are freely given to us of God. which things also we speak, not in the words which man's wisdom, teaches, but which the Holy Ghost teaches comparing spiritual things with spiritual."

The Holy Spirit teaches us comparing spiritual things with (spiritual). Most theologians walk in their flesh and try to explain the miracles of God with their natural minds. Because they lack the Holy Spirit, they refuse to believe in the Supernatural Miracles of God. They try to explain Supernatural Events using their minds and fail miserably. They need Jesus and the Holy Spirit in their hearts and lives to understand the things of God.

Many pastors have refused to allow anyone Holy Spirit filled to teach the Body of Christ how to stand in the Power and Authority we have in Christ. This is why there are brethren sitting in the pews for twenty years and they still don't know how to pray faith prayers, how to be led by the Holy Spirit into Father's will for their lives, how to stand against the Devil, demons, wicked people, and how to be an Overcomer. Many need to be delivered from bondages to sex, alcohol, drugs, fornication, gambling, adultery, perversion, unforgiveness, lust, (covetousness), etc. Many churches are so "user friendly" that they are No Heavenly Good. They are so busy keeping people "comfortable and entertained in their sins and wickedness," that they won't preach any messages on the Wrath of God, on the ungodly. As a result, if Jesus returned today to take up His People, whole churches would be left behind. These wicked pastors will be held accountable for all the souls that perish because they refuse to preach the Truth of The Word of God.

If you are in a church where the Bible isn't read or preached, the Holy Spirit of God is not allowed to move, and the miracles, signs, and wonders of God are not happening, find another church. You don't need to be a member of the (Laodicean) Church that Jesus is going to spew out of His mouth because they are lukewarm.

> Revelation 3:14-22 " Notice the church has plenty of money, plenty of goods and prosperity, and has need of nothing, but they are wretched, and miserable, poor, blind, and naked, in the Spiritual Realm. They are not clothed in white garments (cleansed from their sins). They are filthy and lukewarm in God's sight. They were spiritually blind to the Word of God, living lives of darkness and wickedness, and embracing the world and its lusts. It doesn't say here that they helped the poor, fed the hungry, stood against corruption or did anything right. In verse 20, Jesus was knocking on the door of their hearts trying to get in, but they were not hearing his voice or opening the door to Him.

We need to pray that these deaf and blind ones realize that they need Jesus, not more money, power, or material things. That the love of (mammon) and things would be broken off of them and that they would be passionate for Jesus.

Too many churches and pastors are caught up with owning material things - building bigger buildings, parking lots, condos, building more additions etc. The world's system has gotten ahold of them.

News Flash: Jesus is not returning to take up big buildings or cathedrals. He is coming back for human beings. Reach them for Jesus Christ so they can go to Heaven; not Hell. Do It Now, in Jesus Name! Amen!

CHAPTER 7
THE HOLY SPIRIT

Without the Baptism of the Holy Spirit, A believer in Christ cannot really succeed in the Christian walk. They are Like a car with a flat tire- they can't get very far. Without the Holy Spirit Baptism, they will never fulfill God's full plan for their life. They will be powerless to accomplish much.

When you receive Jesus Christ into your heart as Savior and Lord, you receive Father God and you receive the Holy Spirit who enters your heart and bears witness with your spirit that you are a child of God.

> 2 Corinthians 1:20-22 "For all the promises of God in him are yea, and in him Amen, unto the glory of God by us. Now he which stablished us with you in Christ, and hath anointed us, is God; Who has also (sealed) us, and given the earnest of the Spirit in our hearts."

> Romans 8:8-10 "So then they that are in the flesh cannot please God. But you are not in the flesh, but in the Spirit, if so be that the Spirit of God dwells in you. Now if any man have not the Spirit of Christ, he is none of his. And if Christ be in you, the body is dead because of sin; but the Spirit is life because righteousness." This passage describes being born spiritually as a child of God, but there is much more.

The Baptism of the Holy Spirit is the Power of God released into the believer, enabling them to do the signs, wonders, and miracles as the Holy Spirit moves in them and through them. Without the Baptism of Holy Spirit, the believer has no real power to stand against the demonic forces in the world, effectively. Our flesh profits nothing. The Spirit is Life.

Lets take a look at the gospels and see how many times the Baptism of Holy Spirit is mentioned. In Matthew 3:11-12 John the Baptist said, "I indeed baptize you with water unto repentance; but he that comes after me is mightier than I, whose shoes I am not worthy to bear; he shall baptize you with the Holy Ghost, and with fire.".

Mark 1:7-8 John the Baptist said, "There comes one mightier than I after me, the latchet of whose shoes I am not worthy to stoop and unloose. I indeed have baptized you with water: but he shall baptize you with the Holy Ghost."

Again, the Holy Ghost Baptism by Jesus Christ is mentioned in Luke 3:16 and John 1:29-34. The Holy Ghost Baptism is vital to the believer. Without the Holy Ghost Baptism, the believer cannot possibly get very far. They are like a car that runs out of gas, a dried up tree that bears no fruit, a defenseless person who is spiritually vulnerable to the temptations of life, with no power to resist and fight the devil and win.

When we read about the disciples, we see that when Jesus was taken in the Garden of Gethsemane, they all fled. They were afraid and took off. Peter denied Jesus three times out of fear. They believed in Jesus, walked with Jesus for three years and saw all of the miracles Jesus did, yet they ran away and hid themselves.

Acts 1:3-5 Jesus showed himself alive to his apostles whom he had chosen, being seen of them forty days, and speaking of the things pertaining to the Kingdom of God. And being assembled together with them, commanded them that they should not depart from Jerusalem, but wait for the promise of the Father, which you have heard of me. For John truly baptized with water; but you shall be baptized with the Holy Ghost not many days hence."

In Acts1:8 Jesus said, "But you shall receive power after the Holy Ghost is come upon you: and you shall be witnesses unto me both in Jerusalem, and in Judaea, and in Samaria, and unto the uttermost parts of the Earth."

Notice here, they would receive Power after the Holy Ghost came upon them to reach people for Jesus. Without the Holy Ghost Baptism, you don't have much power to witness to the lost. We need both God's Word and His Holy Spirit Power to witness effectively for Christ with boldness and without fear.

Acts chapter 2:1-4 "And when the day of Pentecost was fully come, they were all with one accord in one place, and suddenly there came a sound from heaven as of a rushing mighty wind, and it filled all the house where they were sitting. And there appeared unto them (cloven) tongues like of fire, and it sat upon each of them, and they were all filled with the Holy Ghost, and began to speak with the other tongues as the Spirit gave them utterance. Everyone heard them speaking in the tongues of different nations." In verse 11 "Crete's and (Arabians), heard them speak in their tongues the wonderful works of God."

Peter, who denied Jesus three times out of fear, now stood up and spoke to the people about Jesus Christ, so powerfully that 3,000 people believed in Jesus. Acts 2:41 Peter no longer feared man, feared what people would think, or hid himself. He was as bold as a lion. The Holy Ghost Baptism gave him the Power to overcome his fears and Preach the Gospel of Jesus Christ.

In Acts Chapter 3:6-8 Peter said to a lame man "In the name of Jesus Christ of Nazareth rise up and walk" and he took the lame man by the right hand and lifted him up and immediately his feet and ankle bones received strength. He lept up, stood, and walked. If Peter hadn't been baptized in the Holy Ghost there would have been no power to heal that man flowing through Peter. Without the Power of Holy Spirit, the man would have stayed lame.

Acts 2:38-39 Peter said, "Repent, and be baptized every one of you in the name of Jesus Christ for the remission of sins, and you shall receive the gift of the Holy Ghost. For the promise is unto you, and to your children, and to all that are afar off, even as many as the Lord our God shall call." The promise is for us and future generations.

As salvation is a Gift of God through Jesus Christ, the Baptism of Holy Spirit is a gift of God that Jesus Christ gives to His body. Both have to be accepted and received to be ours. If we don't accept Jesus Christ as our Savior, we perish. If we don't accept the Baptism of Holy Spirit, we won't have His Power released and operating in our lives.

Acts 8:14-19 Samaria had received the word of God. Peter and John went to Samaria to pray for them that they might receive the Holy Ghost;(for as yet he was fallen upon none of them: only they were baptized in the name of Lord Jesus). Then they laid their hands on them, and they received the Holy Ghost." Notice here that people in Samaria got saved, they got water baptized, but they still needed the Holy Ghost Baptism, laying on of hands.

Acts 19:2-6 There were disciples at Ephesus. Paul said, "Have you received the Holy Ghost since you believed? And they said unto him, we have not so much as heard whether there be any Holy Ghost. And he said unto them unto what then were you baptized? And they said, "Unto John's baptism." Then Paul said, "John baptized with the baptism of repentance, saying unto people, that they should believe in him which should come after him, that is on Christ Jesus."

When they heard this, they were baptized in the name of Lord Jesus. And when Paul had laid his hands upon them, the Holy Ghost came on them and they spoke with tongues and prophesied.

They believed on Jesus, and were water baptized, then Paul laid his hands on them to receive the Holy Ghost Baptism.

If we look at Acts chapter 10 we see a lot of supernatural events occurring.

A man named Cornelius who gave alms to the people and prayed to God saw a vision. An angel of God said, "Your prayers and your alms are come up for a memorial before God." The angel told him to send for Peter. He told him where Peter was staying, at the house of Simon, a tanner. Cornelius, a gentile, not a Jew, sent three people to find Peter.

In the meantime, Peter went up on the roof to pray and fell into a trance. He saw Heaven opened and a great sheet come down with all manner of beasts, birds, creeping things. A voice said to Peter, "Rise, Peter; kill and eat." Peter replied "No Lord, I have never eaten anything that was common and unclean."

There were Old Testament laws about what a Jew could eat and what a Jew couldn't eat because it was considered to be "unclean." Peter had obeyed those laws. A voice spoke unto him again the second time, "What God has cleansed, that call not common." This was done three times and the sheet went back up to heaven. In verse 17 as Peter wondered what the vision meant, the three men, who Cornelius had sent, stood at the gate. The timing of God is always perfect. In verse 19-20 of Acts Chapter 10, "While Peter thought on the vision the Spirit said unto him, 'Behold, three men seek you. Arise and go with them doubting nothing; for I have sent them.'" Notice here, the Holy Spirit spoke to Peter. The men told Peter about Cornelius. In verse 24, we see that Cornelius had called all his relatives and friends together and waited for Peter to come. When Peter came, Cornelius told Peter about the angel who told him to send for Peter. Then Peter said, "Of a truth I perceive that God is no respecter of persons: But in every nation He that fears God and works righteousness, is accepted with him." Then Peter preached the Gospel of Jesus Christ. In verse 44, "While Peter yet spoke, the Holy Ghost fell on them which heard the Word. On the Gentiles also was poured out the gift of the Holy Ghost. For they heard them speak with tongues, and magnify God. Then answered Peter," Can any man forbid water, that these should not be baptized, which have received the Holy Ghost as well as we? And they were water baptized in the name of the Lord."

Notice here, they believed, the Holy Ghost Baptism came upon them, and then they were water baptized. All are very important and vital to the Christian walk with God. Notice that angel visitations, visions, trances, the Holy Spirit speaking to people, Holy Ghost baptisms, speaking in tongues, etc.... are all here in this passage of scripture. All kinds of Supernatural events happened as God's perfect timing invaded human lives.

Peter was of the mindset that all Gentiles were unclean. God spoke to him and changed his heart attitude. Cornelius, a Gentile, was seeking God but had never heard the Gospel of Jesus Christ. He gave money to help people. He fasted and prayed to God. God heard him and sent the Gospel of Salvation to him, his family and his friends. Their lives were all changed. Because Salvation came to the Gentiles, many other Gentiles were witnessed to and got saved. Prior to Cornelius, only Jews were being reached with the Gospel of Jesus Christ.

In Acts Chapter 4:17, the disciples were threatened and ordered not to speak or teach in the name of Jesus. Peter and John answered in verse 19. "Whether it be right In the sight of God to listen to you more than unto God, judge ye. For we cannot but speak the things which we have seen and heard."

After they let them go, the disciples prayed to God, " Behold their threatening: and grant unto your Servants that with all boldness they may speak your word, by stretching forth your hand to heal; and that signs and wonders may be done by the name of your Holy Child Jesus. And when they had prayed, the place was shaken where they were assembled together; and they were all filled with the Holy Ghost, and they spoke the word of God with boldness."These people were baptized with the Holy Spirit in Acts 2, but were refilled with Holy Spirit/ Holy Ghost again. God can refill His people with more of Holy Spirit.

Ephesians 5:18 " And be not drunk with wine, wherein is excess; but be filled with the Spirit; Speaking to yourself in Psalms, and hymns, and spiritual songs, singing and making melody in your hearts to the Lord."

Luke 11:9-13 We can ask for more of Holy Spirit. "And I say unto you, ask, and it shall be given to you; seek, and you shall find; knock and it shall be opened unto you. For everyone that asks receives and he that seeks finds; and to him that knocks it shall be opened. If a son shall ask bread of any of you that is a father, will you give him a stone? Or if he should ask a fish, will you give him a serpent? or if he shall ask an egg, will you instead offer him a scorpion? If you then, being evil, know how to give good gifts unto your children: how much more shall your Heavenly Father give the Holy Spirit to them that ask him?"

God is saying that if you ask for more of the Holy Spirit, you will get more of the Holy Spirit. God will not give you a serpent or scorpion which represent evil spirits. He will give you more of his Holy Spirit, if you ask Him.

Luke 10:19 Jesus said, "Behold, I give unto you power to tread on serpents and scorpions, and over all the power of the enemy; and nothing shall by any means hurt you." The power He is referring to is the Holy Ghost/ Holy Spirit. We will step on and run over serpents and scorpions with the power of Holy Spirit. Holy Spirit will protect us and nothing will be able to harm us.

We all need more of Holy Spirit. In the Old Testament, Elisha asked for a double portion of the spirit that was on Elijah (the Holy Spirit). He received a double portion and signs, wonders and miracles followed his life on Earth. We can keep asking for more of the Holy Spirit. We don't have to settle for just a double portion. We can have an unlimited portion of Holy Spirit, His Power and His (anointing) upon our lives if we just ask Him.

If you have not been baptized in the Holy Spirit through the laying on of a seasoned Believer's hands, you need the Holy Ghost Baptism. Ask Jesus for the Holy Ghost baptism so you will be able to fulfill Father's Will for your life. Without the Holy Spirit Baptism, you will not be able to witness with power, do the greater signs, wonders and miracles and turn this nation and the world back to Jesus. Get the power of God loosed upon your life and you will be unstoppable - the devil's worst nightmare.

Let's look at a few scriptures in the book of Acts where God's Holy Spirit-filled believers ran into a servant of the devil. God's servant won every time.

Acts 6:3, There were many other people filled with the Holy Ghost and wisdom - not just the disciples. In error, some Churches say that the gifts of the Holy Spirit died out with the Apostle's/Disciples. They are completely wrong. Steven and Phillip were not of the original 12 disciples, Yet they were full of wisdom and of the Holy Ghost. Seven more were chosen by the disciples out of many more people, to tend to the food distribution for widows and orphans.

In Acts 5:8 - Acts 7:60, We see that Stephen was full of faith and power. Great wonders and miracles were done by him among the people. The people in the synagogue were not able to resist the wisdom and Spirit by which Stephen spoke. Stephen reminded them of the history of Israel and their forefathers Abraham, Isaac, Jacob, Moses. He reminded them of the false god worship that their forefathers did.

Then Stephen began to rebuke them in Acts 7:51. He called them stiff necked and uncircumcised in heart and ears. You do always resist the Holy Ghost as your fathers did so do you." They hatefully gnashed on him with their teeth. But Stephen was full of the Holy Ghost, looked up into heaven and saw God and Jesus standing at the Father's right hand. They stoned Stephen, who was calling upon God not to charge them with his own murder. Then he died and his spirit and soul went up to heaven.

Saul, who later became the disciple Paul, was there and witnessed the persecution of Stephen, agreeing to it. Later on, Saul repented of his sins against Christ, became a believer known as Paul and wrote many books of the New Testament. He saw Stephen as a man willing to die for Jesus. Later Paul would die for Jesus also.

> Matthew10:18-20 "And you shall be brought before Governors and Kings for my sake, for a testimony against them and the Gentiles. But when they deliver you up, take no thought how or what you shall speak; for it shall be given you in that same hour what you shall speak. For it is not you that speaks, but the Spirit of your Father which speaks in you."

> Acts 16:16-18 "And it came to pass, as we went to prayer, a certain damsel possessed with a spirit of divination met us, which brought her masters much gain by (soothsaying). The same followed Paul and us, and cried saying, "These men are the servants of the most high God, which show unto us the way of Salvation." This she did many days. But Paul, being (grieved), turned and said to the spirit, I command you in the name of Jesus Christ to come out of her. And he came out the same hour."

> Acts 13:6-12 "And when they had gone through the Isle unto Paphos, They found a certain sorcerer, a false prophet, a Jew, whose name was Bar-Jesus; which was with the deputy of the country, Sergius Paulus, a prudent man; who called for Barnabus and Saul, and desired to hear the Word of God. But the sorcerer withstood them, seeking to turn away the deputy from the Faith. Then Saul, who was also called Paul, filled with the Holy Ghost, set his eyes on him, and said, O full of all

subtilty and all mischief, you child of the devil, you enemy of all righteousness, will you not cease to pervert the right ways of the Lord? And now, behold, the hand of the Lord is upon you, and you shall be blind, not seeing the sun for a season. And immediately there fell on him a mist and a darkness; and he went about seeking someone to lead him by the hand. Then the deputy when he saw what was done, believed."

The Holy Spirit spoke to the disciples continually telling them things, teaching them things, directing and guiding them into Father's Will and purposes.

In Acts 8:26-40, First" the angel of the Lord spoke to Philip, saying, Arise, and go toward the South unto the way that goes down from Jerusalem to Gaza which is Desert. And he arose and went; and behold, a man of Ethiopia, a eunuch of great authority under Candace Queen of the Ethiopians was returning. He was sitting in his chariot reading Isaiah 53:7 (Esaias in Hebrew).

The Holy Spirit said unto Phillip, "go near and join yourself to the chariot." Philip heard the eunuch reading the scriptures. He wanted to know who the scriptures were about. So Philip preached Jesus unto him. All of a sudden there was water, in the desert, where the eunuch could be water baptized believing that Jesus Christ is the Son of God. They both went down into the water and Phillip baptized him. And when they came up out of the water, the Spirit of the Lord caught away Philip, that the eunuch saw him no more; and he went on his way rejoicing. But Phillip was found at Azotus (approximately 28 miles from Gaza). He was transported by the Holy Spirit. Through the Ethiopian eunuch, the Gospel of Jesus Christ got into Ethiopia.

I don't know about you, but I desire the Holy Spirit to transport me, where God wants me. What a wonderful way to get where you need to be. How exciting.

Holy Spirit transported The prophet Elijah quite frequently. Kings 2:9-17 When Elijah went up by a whirlwind into heaven, in the chariot of fire, other prophets in versus 16- 17 thought maybe the Spirit of the Lord had taken him up to some mountaintop or into some valley. It was public knowledge that Holy Spirit did transport Elijah at times.

In 1 Kings 18:12, Obadiah Said to Elijah, "And it shall come to pass, as soon as I am gone from you, that the Spirit of the Lord shall carry you where I know not.

If you study the book of Acts you will see that the Holy Spirit spoke to them, Angels appeared and spoke to them, and they were filled with the Holy Spirit many times, not just once at Pentecost. Holy Spirit led them, informed them, guided them, etc.... Without the Holy Ghost Baptism, you are missing out on all of the supernatural things God wants to do in you and through you. You will never be able to fulfill your God-given Destiny without the Holy Ghost Baptism. Ask Jesus for it now.

CHAPTER 8
WARNINGS OF THE HOLY SPIRIT AND POWER OF HOLY SPIRIT

In 1999, I was going back to Africa to preach in Kenya, Uganda, Tanzania, Rwanda, Burundi, and Zaire/Congo. It would be a 2 ½ month trip. One day, before I left for Africa, I was praying about these African Nations and got a check in my spirit over Zaire/Congo. Holy Spirit was warning me not to go there. I wrote my coordinator in Kenya a letter telling him not to schedule anything in Zaire. He never got my letter. When I arrived in Kenya and looked at the schedule, Zaire was on it. Immediately I got a check in my spirit about Zaire. After preaching the weeks in Kenya, Uganda, Tanzania, Rwanda and Burundi, Holy Spirit spoke to me. An overwhelming feeling of grief hit me and I knew if I went to Zaire, I would never see my family again on planet earth. I would die.

The Kenyan pastors, I was traveling with, were going to head to Zaire. I said, " Please drive me to the Burundi airport. I'll take a plane back to Kenya. God is warning me that if I go to Zaire I will be killed." They all decided to drive back to Kenya with me. The next day, they heard a report that three Americans and five Uganda college students were murdered in the forest, by Congolese Terrorists who fled back into the Congo. They were studying the gorillas, in the forest, when they were murdered. If we went to Zaire, we would have had to pass through that forest. We would have been among the dead. Holy Spirit saved Our Lives.

Acts 16: 6-10 "Now when they (Paul and Silas) had gone throughout Phrygia and the region of Galatia, and were forbidden of the Holy Ghost to preach word in Asia. After they were come to Mysia, they purposed to go into Bithynia, but the Spirit suffered them not. And after passing by Mysia came down to Troas. And a vision appeared to Paul in the night: There stood a man of Macedonia, and prayed him, saying, "Come over into Macedonia and help us."

As we can see here, they were guided by Holy Spirit. Asia was not ready to hear the gospel, at that time. If they had disobeyed Holy Spirit and had gone to Asia, they probably would have died there. The Holy Spirit told them not to go into Bithynia. Then they saw the Macedonia vision and went there.

In 1990, my Husband Paul was going on a business trip. He was flying from the airport near us to the New York City Airport. From there he was flying to Texas. As usual, I took him to the local airport, but Holy Spirit warned me that if Paul got on the plane, he would die. An overwhelming feeling of grief came over me and I knew something was wrong with the plane. I begged him not to get on the plane. He said, " I have to. I'll miss my connecting flight." In tears, I walked away and prayed. " Father God, send an angel to open the eyes of whoever is checking out the plane. Let them see what is wrong with it and let it not leave the ground, in Jesus name, Amen." About five minutes before they were to board the plane, an announcement came over the intercom, " This flight is cancelled due to major mechanical failure." Limos arrived to drive the passengers to New York City. The plane that had major mechanical failure was a small 14 to 20 passenger plane. One man was screaming at the girl behind the desk, "I'll miss my connecting flight!" I yelled, in a loud voice, " I thank God that plane didn't take off. You would all be dead." Then the man shut up. Paul was driven by limousine to the New York City Airport, upgraded to an earlier flight and arrived at the Texas Airport earlier than he would have arrived otherwise. God is good! After this plane incident, Paul received Jesus as his Savior and Lord that same year, 1990.

Usually, I didn't fast when leaving on a six-week-long preaching/ mission trip to Africa. The Lord wanted me to be strong, not weakened in my body, from fasting. But one trip to Kenya was different. The week before I was to leave, the Lord had me fast for five days, eat for 2 days, and leave for Kenya. I only had liquids for 5 days, no solid food. Once I arrived in Kenya, I realized why.

The day after I arrived, my coordinator and I were walking down the street in Nairobi, to buy Some Bibles to take into the villages. People, in the distance, were running back and forth zigzagging all over the place trying to avoid someone or something. As we approached, we saw a 4 ft tall woman, full of demons, chasing people through the streets. She was out of her mind, in dirty rags, demanding money of people and climbing on people's backs. She started toward me. I pointed my finger at her and said "In the name of Jesus," and she fell to the ground. The Lord said, "It is Legion." Legion means that she had thousands of demons in her. I said, " Legion, in the name of Jesus, come out of her." They began manifesting as long strands of mucus coming out of her nose and puke coming out of her mouth. They were running out of her. It took less than eight minutes and they were all gone. My coordinator Chris interpreted for me as I asked her some questions. She had been in the marketplace three years sleeping outside, in the gutter. She was from a town miles away. I preached Jesus Christ to her and she received Jesus into her heart and life. People were amazed to see her in her right mind, walking with us. I took her to my hotel room, let her wash in the shower, and gave her a skirt and blouse to wear. Then I brought her some food and a bus ticket to go back home. I told her to get into a church where Jesus is preached and Holy Spirit is present. She needed to read the Bible and press into God to keep the demons from trying to return.

After this incident, I realized that I had to fast that time because certain demons only come out by prayer and fasting. An entire Legion of demons had to bow before the Name of Jesus and had to leave her right away, when I commanded them to, in Jesus name. Every knee will bow to Jesus. Even Satan himself must bow to My Jesus. Satan is just a fallen angel. Jesus created the angels.

While in Rwanda and Burundi, a pastor interpreted for me into French. He told me that many Rwandan pastors had been killed in a plane crash. He was supposed to go with them, on this trip, but he got a check in his spirit, that something was wrong. Holy Spirit warned him not to go. He didn't go, and his life was spared. I am sure Holy Spirit warned the other pastors too, but they did not listen. A fog came up, the pilot couldn't see, and the plane hit the side of a mountain. All aboard were killed. Listening to Holy Spirit can save your life.

There were a few times when Holy Spirit told me I wasn't safe in a hotel. One time my interpreter Ben, coordinator Chris and I arrived in a town. The hotel was a separate building from the restaurant that was across the parking lot from the hotel. My coordinator, Chris was tired and went to his room. I went to my room. My interpreter, Ben, was hungry, so he went across to eat in the restaurant.

While in my room, I had no peace. I couldn't sleep and felt something was wrong. I rebuked the devil, thinking it was the enemy trying to rob my sleep. I still had no peace. When I asked the Lord why I had no peace, Holy Spirit said, " You are not safe here. In the morning, change hotels."

The next morning I bathed and got dressed. Then I knocked at the coordinator's door and said, " Pack up your things, we have to change hotels." He was annoyed because he had just unpacked for the week. I knocked at my interpreter's door and told him we had to change hotels. He said, " It is good we are getting out of here. .While at the restaurant, I overheard the owner of the place talking to another guy trying to figure out whether to call the police or not. His daughter had just been kidnapped by gangsters who were holding her for ransom." I would have been their next victim, had I stayed there. Most Africans have the idea that anyone with white skin has a lot of money or can get a lot of money. That is why it's important to listen to Holy Spirit's warnings. We changed hotels.

There were times Holy Spirit warned me not to cut across a field to get to the post office, to call home. Sometimes I would be in the villages for weeks. There were no phones, cell phones, computers, mailmen etc.… When I got back to Kisumu, Kenya, I would eagerly head to the post office to phone Paul. I obeyed the Holy Spirit when he told me not to cut across the fields. There could have been a poisonous snake there or someone hiding in the tall grass to ambush me. I walked on the roadway instead. It took a few more minutes, but I was kept safe from harm.

Sometimes Holy Spirit can reveal to you the real heart of someone around you. One time, while preaching in a village church, a woman in the church came up to me and said, "Sister Kathy, I am so glad you are here." When I looked into her eyes , I saw something demonic glaring at me and realized she was into witchcraft.

Matthew 6:22 "The light of the body is the eye: If therefore your eye be single, your whole body shall be full of light. But if your eye be evil, your whole body shall be full of darkness. If therefore the light that is in you be darkness, how great is the darkness." I always Look into people's eyes to see if I see the Light of Christ in them.

This same woman came up to me with a package wrapped in newspapers. She said, "Sister Kathy, I got you a present." Immediately Holy Spirit warned me it was evil. Under my breath, I bound the demons in it. When I opened it, I saw two African heads made out of clay. She had made them with spells, incantations, witchcraft and demons attached. She figured I would carry them with me everywhere I went and the demons would attack me and prevent me from accomplishing anything. After she walked away, my coordinator took them to an outhouse and threw them down into the outhouse hole with the poop where they belonged.

Sometimes people's eyes can be full of false light. They can shine with some kind of weird illumination from attending New Age Movement, demonic festivals where strange music is played and some kind of crazy lights and demons are released. They believe the lie that they are going to "evolve into gods." It is the same lie Satan told Adam and Eve, in the garden, before they ate the forbidden fruit.

Genesis 3:4-5 " The snake said unto the woman, "You shall not surely die. For God knows that in the day you eat thereof, then your eyes shall be opened, and you shall be as Gods, knowing Good and Evil." The New Age Movement is Satan's old lie with a new packaging. Don't be deceived. The real light is Jesus Christ, the Word of God.

Paul, Brian, and I, met a man who conducts these demonic New Age light shows, when we attended a poetry reading event. When we tried to tell him about Jesus, he said a belief in God was ridiculous. He talked about some kind of weird four dimensions. After walking away from him, we prayed against Satan, his four dimensions of lies and occult practices and spiritual blindness. The man doesn't realize the darkness he is in and is promoting. Sadly, he is so intellectually wrong no one can get through to him with the Gospel of Jesus Christ. He said it is archaic to believe in God and he would not engage in such an unintelligent conversation. Some day he will stand before the God he refused. His fake light will not save his soul from hell. Jesus Saves. Without Jesus there is no Salvation.

Not all bad dreams come from the devil. Sometimes Holy Spirit warns people in dreams about what Satan is planning to do. If they pray against it, they can dismantle it before it happens. For example, a woman in Kenya, had a dream that her daughter's car collided with a sugarcane truck. She saw the car destroyed in the dream, and knew her daughter was injured. She should have said " Satan, in Jesus name, your plans to destroy my daughter's car and injure my daughter in a collision with a sugar truck are canceled, null and void and will not happen in Jesus name. Amen." She didn't pray against it, a few weeks later, it happened.

In a Village, my coordinator had a dream that people jumped out of the bushes and were dragging us away somewhere, against our will. When he told me about the dream, I prayed, " in Jesus name, I cancel the devil and his agent's plans to have people kidnap or attack us, or drag us off somewhere, or harm us. These plans are canceled, null and void. This will not happen, in Jesus name. Amen." Because we prayed against it, it did not happen.

If you have a dream about an accident, an illness attacking a loved one, someone attacking a loved one or you, a bad thing happening... pray against it and dismantle it, in Jesus name. As a child of God, we can stop the enemy before his plans can manifest if we pray against them and cancel them , in Jesus name.

When Holy Spirit warns you about someone or tells you not to go somewhere, or about an object, Listen and Obey him. He is trying to protect your life. If it wasn't for Holy Spirit, I would have been wiped out by our enemy the devil, and his agents, many years ago.

The Holy Spirit can warn you not to purchase an object, a piece of jewelry, an item of clothing, a certain antique, etc. . if there is a demonic spirit or demonic anointing on it.

> Acts 19:11 "And God wrought special miracles by the hands
> of Paul; So that from his body were brought unto the sick
> handkerchiefs or aprons, and the diseases departed from
> them, and the evil spirits went out of them."

Paul would lay his hands on the handkerchiefs and aprons, and impart a Holy Spirit anointing into them. That anointing when brought to the sick, healed them. People would carry the Holy Spirit's anointed cloths to their sick family members and they would recover.

As the Holy Spirit Anointing can be imparted into objects by God's People, a demonic spirit and demonic anointing can be imparted into objects by Satan's people.

Years ago, my mother phoned me from another state to tell me that my sister was seeing things moving in her room. Her blood cells were all at crazy levels and she was in horrible pain.

When I heard that she was seeing things moving in her room, I knew she was under demonic attack. After packing my suitcase, I drove for four hours praying in tongues (Holy Spirit's Language), and arrived at the house. Tongues is one of the giftings given to the Body of Christ mentioned in 1 Corinthians Chapters 12 and 14.

When I don't know how to pray for someone, what to pray, what is really going on with them, what is attacking them, etc...I ask Holy Spirit to give me the right prayer that needs to be prayed. The Holy Spirit knows what the situation really is, what needs to be prayed, and how to help the person effectively. He is God the Holy Spirit. He knows it all and sees it all. I don't. I pray in my Holy Spirit Prayer Language until I have peace in my heart. Then I know it will be OK.

In the middle of the night, the Lord led me to go into my sister's room. There was a white spirit form moving at the foot of her bed. I said, "I bind you in the Name of Jesus and cast you out of this house never to return again." It vanished. Then I prayed, "Lord show me what is causing this attack on my sister."

My sister's boyfriend had purchased a piece of artwork from a local roadside stand and gave it to my sister. The painting was of a black panther with it's teeth barred waiting to bite someone. It was hanging on her bedroom wall.

When I asked the Lord to show me anything demonic that I needed to stand against, I was shocked to see a spirit form go over the face of the panther. It's green eyes began moving and its teeth began moving up and down as it's jaw opened and closed. I jumped back a few feet and said ,"Lord, what do you want me to do with this?" The Lord said, "Burn it." I said, "Lord, if I burn her painting and she gets angry, how am I to lead her to You?"

The Lord said , "Take it outside and put it under the tree." I went forward, grabbed the painting, turned the back of the frame toward me (the face away from me), marched it outside and threw it under the tree.

I went back into my sister's room and asked the Lord if there was anything else. He said, "No." Then the Lord had me anoint my sister with oil and pray for the healing of her body and her Salvation, in Jesus Name. The next day, she was no longer in pain and I was able to lead her in a Salvation Prayer to receive Jesus.

I told her the painting was demonic and to burn it. Instead, she gave it back to her boyfriend. He put it on his wall above his tropical fish tank. In the morning, the fish were all dead floating belly up in the water. He got frightened and threw the painting in the back seat of his car.

Unknown to my sister, she borrowed the car to drive my nephew to pick up a cat someone had promised him. She told my nephew what I said about the painting. The car ran out of gas and they had to walk several miles to get a gas can. The gasoline gauge in the car said they had gas, Yet it ran out of gas. . While driving, a dog came out of no where and ran into the side of the car. My nephew noticed the painting in the back seat . Needless to say, they lit a fire and burnt it up by the side of the road.

> Deuteronomy 7:25-26 says, "The graven images of their gods shall you burn with fire: you shall not desire the silver or gold that is on them, not take it unto you, lest you be snared, for it is an abomination to the Lord your God, Neither shall you bring an abomination into your house, lest you be a cursed thing like it: but you shall utterly detest it, and you shall utterly abhor it: for it is a cursed thing."

> In 1Corinthians 2:11-14, we see that the Holy Spirit compares spiritual things with spiritual. Someone who does not have the Holy Spirit, does not see what things really are. With my natural eyes, in my flesh, I couldn't see what was wrong with my sister's painting. When I asked Holy Spirit to show me, He opened up my spiritual vision to see what was really there. Holy Spirit reveals what is really of God and what is not of God.

The world promotes Ouija boards. People ignorantly buy them and allow their children to play with them. They don't realize that a demonic spirit moves and answers their questions. It's object is to destroy your children. There was a college honor student who began playing with a Ouija board. She became depressed, her grades dropped, and she had a total mental breakdown.

People allow their children to have witchcraft books, watch wizard movies, read wizard books, watch demonic murderous horror films, practice witchcraft, enchantments, tarot card reading, seances (necromance), etc... All these things are listed in Deuteronomy 18:9-12 as "Abominations to God."

When you bring objects that are connected with these things into your house, you are welcoming Satan and his demons to come in and attack you, your family, your marriage, your finances, your health, etc...

Years ago, there were silver statues of wizards and dragons sold in local stores. People were buying them, not realizing that they were bringing Abominations into their homes.

> In Revelation12:9, Satan himself is described as "the great dragon, that old serpent." The Chinese people worship the red dragon. They don't realize they are actually worshipping Satan.

Karl Marx who invented the "Communist" and "Socialist" ideologies was a Satanist. These Wicked Ideologies are designed to deny God, deny Christ, deny the Bible, deny God Given Freedoms, liberty, justice, kindness, goodness, decency, righteousness, truth, self-will, etc... Marx was possessed by Satan.

These Wicked Marxist ideologies are used by Satanists to control entire populations of people with intimidation, oppression, threats of death, persecutions, beatings, imprisonments, murders, tyranny, misery. Anyone who opposes these Satanists is tortured, imprisoned, and put to death. Communism shows no mercy, no genuine love, no compassion, no tolerance for any opposition etc... Under Socialism, the Government owns Everything. It owns the people it rules over,. body, soul, and spirit, and demands total obedience to it or death. It demands that People worship IT, instead of God. A Communist Government demands the Worship of Everyone it Governs. No one can own a house, pick the job they want, get rewards and raises for working hard, enjoy the fruits of their labor, etc. They control the entire brain washing of the children into their demonic mindsets and sick ideologies.

If you are a Christian and agree with any of these demonic ideologies, you have been deceived by Satan. Our freedoms, liberties, talents, abilities, giftings, free-will and our very lives are all gifts from God. They do not come from government at all. Read the Bible and discover God's Truth. If you know God's Truth, you won't be deceived by Satan's lies.

The Holy Spirit is God The Holy Spirit. He knows what Satan is up to and can warn you, ahead of time, of any and all danger. If you obey Him, He can save your life.

I had a cousin who had been addicted to alcohol and drugs. He came to faith in Jesus, was attending a Salvation Army Church, and was doing well.

One day, an old friend approached him and convinced him to go off with him. The old friend was still addicted to drugs and had purchased some. I'm sure the Holy Spirit tried to warn my cousin not to go with that old friend. He didn't listen.

My cousin was found dead a few days later from a drug overdose. Satan will always tempt you in the thing God delivered you from. If it is lust, he will tempt you to watch lustful TV programs, soaps, porn, computer sex sites etc...

If it is alcohol, drugs, gambling, etc..., he will tempt you, using people to try to lure you back to them.

We are to flee temptation. If you try to resist it by being exposed to it, you will be snared by it. Get away from it. Don't be around it.

Flee Temptation and resist the devil and he will flee from you. First draw near to God. He will give you all the strength and power you need to fight the devil. Listen to and obey Holy Spirit when He warns you. It may save your life.

CHAPTER 9
GIFTS OF THE HOLY SPIRIT

The gifts of Holy Spirit are all available to us today. They did not die out with the original apostles and the other seventy mentioned in Luke 10:1-19, as some mistaken churches teach.

God's Holy Spirit and God's Power have not diminished. He is the same yesterday, today and forever. The same signs, wonders and miracles mentioned in the Book of Acts, I have seen God do through me. If He can manifest His gifts and power through me, He can do it through you also. He is no respecter of persons. Whoever is surrendered to God and available for His Divine purposes, He will use mightily.

The devil will tell you that you are too young, too old, not ready, not educated enough, you haven't attended a certain Bible College, you don't have the man-made pedigree papers on your wall, etc.... If Almighty God, who knows all things, says you are ready, you are ready. Step out in faith and watch the Lord move mightily in you and through you.

When I asked Holy Spirit whether or not I should attend Bible College, He said, "I AM Your Teacher." He is God the Holy Spirit. He wrote the Bible. Yes, He used people to put down on parchments His Words, but the Words were God's Words. He has been my teacher all these years. When Holy Spirit opens up the scriptures to you, you have the real, untarnished Word of God. Man's tainted opinions, ideas, and vain imaginings are not in the way. The Holy Spirit gives you the real meaning of the Word of God and opens the eyes of your spiritual understanding, to understand the deeper things of God. Holy Spirit compares spiritual things with spiritual and can show you things to come.(John 16:13).

Read the Bible and be taught and led by the Holy Spirit. Weigh everything you hear any human speak by the Word of God. If it is contrary to God's Word, it is the devil's lie. Read the Bible for yourself and allow the Holy Spirit to teach you His Spiritual Truths.

> 1 Corinthians chapters 12 and 14, mention the Spiritual Gifts that are available to us. There are many gifts and variations of gifts but they all come from the Holy Spirit.

If we look at the healing evangelists, we see a difference in their healing giftings. For example, Oral Roberts would lay his hands on people and they would receive their healing. Marilyn Hickey gets a Word of Knowledge from Holy Spirit as to what illnesses the Lord is going to heal. She may speak, "The Lord is healing tumors." People began Praising God as their tumors, cysts, and growths disappear. Benny Hinn conducts beautiful worship services and the Healing Power of God manifests and people are healed. Each one operates in a variation of a healing gift.

If we read about the Azusa Street Revival that took place over a hundred years ago, there were certain people used to pray over certain illnesses. One person was anointed to pray for missing teeth to be restored and they grew back. Another person was anointed to pray for hair to grow back. Bald people received hair. Another was anointed to pray over a missing leg and a leg and foot and toes grew back. The man had been hobbling around on a peg leg for years. The top of his leg got infected. They removed the peg, and prayed over the stump. The leg, foot and toes grew out. Nothing is impossible for our God. These are just some of the miracles mentioned in the "Azusa They Told Me Their Stories" book by J. Edward Morris. Many other miracles happened there. What God did then, He can do today, with us.

> In 1 Corinthians 12:8, "The Word of Wisdom" and "The Word of Knowledge", are both listed as gifts of the Holy Spirit. Sometimes Holy Spirit can give you an information download that is needed in a particular situation. He can make you aware of something you were never told about in order to help someone. I'll give you an example of this.

One day we met my Husband's Cousin and his wife and three year old child at a barbeque. They had many other children who were not traveling with them, at the time. They had come on vacation from the west coast. We are on the east coast. We heard that their son had a heart problem. They went back home and we heard nothing about them for over three years.

One day Paul's cousin came to our house and asked if he could stay with us for four months, until he could find a job and get settled. He got a job, worked and lived with us for five months. He was separated from his wife for three years. He would phone her, argue with her, and hang up. We did not know the cause of their marriage break up.

He would say to me, ""You remind me of my wife, Your faith and her faith are similar." I realized his wife knew Jesus as her Savior and Lord. I began praying that the Lord would heal their marriage.

One day Paul's cousin came home early from work. I heard God say ,"Ask him to come upstairs and have some tea." When he came upstairs, for tea, the Lord said, "Ask him if it was after the death of his son that he and his wife split up."

When I asked him, his face got red and he screamed," My wife didn't love our son as much as I did. She wasn't as upset as I was when he died." He yelled for a while. When he calmed down, I said, "You say that my faith and your wife's faith are similar. The devil has been lying to you telling you that your wife didn't love your son as much as you did. Your wife believes that your son is up in heaven with Jesus and some day, when she physically dies, she will see him again.

Because she has prayed and the Lord is comforting her, upholding her, giving her strength, and healing her broken heart, she doesn't appear to be as upset as you are. You are angry with God, blaming God for your son's death, angry with everything and everyone, and the devil has lied to you and separated you from your wife and other children. You need to repent, trust God with your son and ask Him to comfort you and help you with this. IF you let Him, He will comfort you as He did for your wife."

Shortly after the truth was spoken to him, Paul's cousin quit his job, went back home, began dating his wife, and renewed his wedding vows with her. The Lord put their marriage and their lives back together. His wife got her husband back and his other children got their dad back. Praise God!

1 Corinthians 12:9 The Holy Spirit gives us faith. We can ask for more faith to believe. We can ask for the gift of Faith to believe that the impossible is possible with God. I have said, Father God, I don't just want small mustard seed faith that moves mountains, Give me Mountainous Faith that moves Kingdoms."

I have seen a dead boy raised , from the dead and brought back to life in Buteri, Kenya, storms leave our area, a wall of turbulence removed 20 feet away from the plane, tumors vanish, cancers shrink, barren wombs opened, broken bones healed in seconds, diseases healed, demoniacs delivered, bondages broken, etc. by the Power of God.

1Corinthians12:10-11 "But all these work that one and the selfsame Spirit, dividing to every man severally as he will." Holy Spirit gives the gifts as He wills.

Paul goes on to speak about the Body of Christ and the fact that there are many members. If the foot shall say, "Because I am not the hand, I am not of the body"; is it not of the body? If the whole body were an eye, where would be the hearing? In verse 18 Paul says ,"But now God set the members every one of them in the body, as it pleases Him."

1 Corinthians 12:28 "And God has set some in the church, first apostles, secondarily prophets, thirdly teachers, after that miracles, then gifts of healing, helps, governments, diversities of tongues."

Ephesians 4:11 "And He gave some, apostles, and some, prophets: and some, evangelists; and some pastors and teachers; For the perfecting of the saints, for the work of the ministry, for the edifying of the body of Christ: Till we all come in the unity of the faith, and of the knowledge of the Son of God, unto a perfect man, unto the measure of the fulness of Christ."

Notice that these five folds of ministry are to work in building the body of Christ into the unity of the faith and the knowledge of the Son of God (Jesus Christ).

Sadly, here in the Northeast, very few churches allow all five folds of ministry to function and impart their portions to the believers. In most churches, only the pastor is functioning, and he won't allow the other four folds to preach to the body of Christ. That is why the sheep are suffering from a lack of knowledge, engaged in sins, hurting from past wounds, suffering from addictions, under nourished, under fed, unable to Stand in Faith, unable to pray Faith Prayers, harboring unforgiveness in their hearts, not knowing how to Fight The Good Fight of Faith and Be An Overcomer, etc... God will hold these Pastors accountable for their selfish ambitions that hinder the sheep from growing spiritually in the things of God.

Get Baptized in the Holy Ghost and desire spiritual gifts. If you use the ones you have, God will entrust you with more. If you are faithful in the small things, God will give you greater things. Study your Bible. Know what God says is right and wrong. Weigh everything by what God says. Set your mind and value system on God's Mind and Value System.

There are (so-called) Christian Churches that are so compromised with the world that there is no difference between them and the world. These are really Satan's Churches that condone everything that God's Holy Bible says is sin, is wrong, and is wicked. Read the Bible and see if your pastor is really a pastor of God or not. Weigh what he teaches by what God's Word says. See if he agrees with God or is standing with the devil. Your soul is at stake. Know what God's Word really says and obey God.

Holy Spirit can reveal to you what is going on in someone's heart that is blocking their physical healing. Here are some examples:

Once I saw a woman, attending a church service, that was all bent over. The Lord said, "She has a lot of unforgiveness in her heart and it is weighing her down and bending her over." I went up to the woman and asked, "Is there anyone you haven't really forgiven?" She said, "My daughter ran off with a man I didn't like and my son stole my money and used it to buy drugs." I said, "You must be willing to forgive them and let that unforgiveness and bitterness go. If you don't let it go, our Heavenly Father won't forgive you of your sins." She refused to let the unforgiveness go, and remained bent over. She could have been totally healed spiritually, emotionally, and physically.

Once I sought the Lord to heal a brother in a Church I was attending. He was becoming crippled in his legs. I prayed an entire week for him and he looked worse. I fasted and prayed the next week and he was worse. I said, "Lord, I prayed in faith, for his healing. I asked in Jesus Name for him to be healed. Why haven't you healed him?" Holy Spirit said, "Unless he forgives his brother George, I cannot bless his unforgiveness by healing him."

We see here that the reason some people don't receive their physical healing is their refusal to forgive the people who have wronged them. God cannot bless unforgiveness. We must forgive .

> In Matthew 6:14-15 Jesus said, "For if you forgive men their trespasses, your heavenly Father will also forgive you: But if you do not forgive men their trespasses, neither will your Father forgive your trespasses."

If a person loves their unforgiveness more than they love Jesus, their unforgiveness becomes their false God. It destroys them, their lives and innocent people around them, if they refuse to let it go. It causes a lot of breast cancers because it lodges in the hearts of human beings. It blocks the blessings of God from a person's life and keeps them in bondage to the past and whatever happened back then. They are not free to enjoy their present and their future.

> In Matthew 18:21-35, the King forgave a person a huge debt. The person who was forgiven much, refused to forgive another person of a smaller debt. When the King found out, in verse 34, the one who refused to forgive was released to tormentors. Tormentors are demonic spirits that keep reminding the person what happened. They keep the memories of that past event fresh in the present, torment the person with nightmares, dreams, etc...That is why you meet people who can relate past, horrible events, like they happened today. They haven't forgiven the people involved, let it go and moved on with their lives. All of the emotional pain, heartbreak, memories, hurt, rejection, nasty words spoken to them etc... are still there every day-ruining their present and future.

Let God remove the junk from your heart so you can be free to enjoy your present and future. God wants you to be healthy in body, soul, and spirit.

When a believer is Baptized in the Holy Spirit, they usually get a prayer language called tongues. Tongues is a prayer language of a nation of people, in another country, or an angelic language. It is very necessary in situations where you have a burden in your heart for someone or something and you don't really know how to pray what is needed. The Holy Spirit always knows what needs to be prayed at any given time. He is God the Holy Spirit. He knows it all. We don't. By Praying in Tongues until we have peace in our hearts, we can be assured that the matter is settled correctly.

The Disciple Paul said in 1 Corinthians 14:15, "What is it then? I will pray with the spirit, and I will pray with my understanding also: I will sing with the spirit, and I will sing with the understanding also." He did both. It is exciting when you sing a song in your prayer language to God and all of a sudden you sing the same song in your own language so you know what you have been singing.

There is a gift of Prophesy that gives guidance and direction to the Body of Christ. It must be carefully judged by the leaders to make sure it lines up with the Word of God. There are true Prophets of God, and there are false prophets of Baal.

In 1 Kings 18:17-40 Elijah was God's real prophet. Jezebel, the wicked witch, had 450 fake prophets of Baal and another 400 fake prophets of the groves of trees. Yes, they worshipped trees. Elijah had a show down on Mount Carmel with the false prophets. The false gods of the false prophets didn't answer them. They called upon Baal from morning to night and he didn't answer. They even sliced their skin with lancets to give their false god a blood sacrifice, but he didn't answer them. Anyone who makes cuttings on their skin, sacrifices children by shedding their innocent blood, etc...does not serve the real God. They have a false God.

At the time of the evening sacrifice to God, Elijah set the stone altar, put the wood on it, and laid the animal sacrifice upon it. Then he doused the entire thing with many buckets of water over and over again. When he called upon the Lord, the Lord answered by fire and burnt up everything. People fell on their faces and said, "The Lord, He is God!" Read the Bible for yourself. It's Amazing! Anytime there is a contest between our God and false gods, our God wins.

In my walk with Jesus, real prophets of God have been used by God, to confirm to me that I have been truly hearing God's direction for my life. For example, in 1996 while on a CBN Tour of Israel, Michael Little prophesied over me , "There is healing in your hands. God is sending you all over the world." The Holy Spirit came upon me and I couldn't remain standing. That is a normal occurrence. If you read about Solomon's Temple Dedication, the Glory of God filled the place and the priests couldn't stand up to minister. They were on the floor.

In 1997, after a mission trip to Africa with Marilyn Hickey Ministries, the Lord was showing me that I was to go back to Africa. My Bible kept falling open and scriptures kept leaping at me from the pages. It was like they were highlighted just for me. "I will make the way for you. I will cause you to speak My Words. I will be your front guard. I will be your rear guard, enemies will rise against you but I will fight them. I have called you and set you apart for such a time as this."

One day a visiting pastor, and an intercessor and a prophetess came from Long Island to a church I was attending. I never met them before and they never met me. I said, "Lord, if you want me to go back to Africa to do crusades and preach in churches, confirm it to me out of the mouth of this prophetess."

After the service, I went up to the prophetess and said, "Can you pray for me?" She began with, "There is healing in your hands. God is sending you all over the world (the same words Michael Little spoke over me in Israel). Then she said, "I will go before you. I will cause you to speak my words. Enemies will rise against you but I will fight them. I have called you and set you apart for such a time as this. This is confirmation." I had no more doubts, questions, or hesitation. I wired funds to a total stranger I had met, who attended Jesus Celebration Center Church in Kenya, to organize crusades for me. In faith I got on a plane to do crusades when I had never preached before in my life. In faith, my Husband Paul released me to go. People thought we were both nuts, but we were both hearing from God.

The first message I preached was at Kisumu Medical College "You Must be Born Again to enter the Kingdom of God" Seventeen college students received Jesus as their Savior and Lord. Praise the Lord!

The Lord took me from crusades, to preaching His Word in churches, to huge camp meetings, to Jesus is Lord Radio , and Sayre Voice of Mercy Radio and TV out of Eldoret, Kenya.

One day, before I ever left for Kenya, a false prophetess came up to me. She said, "The Lord wants you to be a missionary to Germany. I'll teach you German." The Holy Spirit bore no witness to her words. I realized she was Satan's false messenger, trying to lead me in a wrong direction. A real prophet/prophetess of God will agree with what the Lord has already been showing you. If there is any check in your spirit don't believe them.

Many young women, in Kenya, have been deceived into marrying young men who approached them saying, "Thus saith the Lord, you're going to be my wife.." I warned the girls that if the Lord hadn't told them to marry those young men, the young men were false prophets who didn't even know the Lord at all. To say, "Thus saith the Lord", when God did not say it, they are in danger of death. They have no reverence or fear of God at all.

> 1 Corinthians 12:10 lists "discerning of spirits" as one of the gifts of the Holy Spirit. It is important that we ask the Lord for this gift. There are a lot of "spiritual things" going on now, that are Not Of God.

> 2 Acts 16:16-18 tells of a girl who was following the disciples around every day saying, "These men are the servants of God, which show unto us the way of salvation." I believe there was a demon trying to annoy them through her. Finally, Paul commanded it to come out of her and it left.

Not everything or everyone spiritual is of God. Once I was on a plane heading to Africa, when a man wearing a priests collar sat next to me. I said, "Are you a pastor?" He said, "I pastor a church in Ghana. He told me I should get a certain book by an author that had " deeper insight into the Holy Spirit." He denied that Jesus Christ was the Word of God who became flesh and dwelt among us.

Holy Spirit reminded me of 1 John4 :1-3, "Beloved, believe not every spirit, but try the spirits whether they be of God: because many false prophets are gone out into the world. Hereby know the Spirit of

God: Every spirit that confesses that Jesus Christ is come in the flesh is of God: and every spirit that denies that Jesus Christ is come in the flesh is not of God: and this is the spirit of anti-Christ, whereof you have heard that it should come: and even now already it is in the world." I pointed my finger in his face (the finger next to my thumb) and said, "You are a cult leader and are leading a cult. Repent and burn that other book and get back to preaching the Bible, the Word of God. The devil has deceived you into denying that Jesus , the Word of God , became flesh and dwelt among us".

If I didn't read my Bible and know the scriptures, I would have been deceived by this man who was teaching demonic lies, instead of God's Truths. Read your Bible. Know what God's Word says. Otherwise, you can easily be deceived into believing Satan's lies.

Another time, I was on a plane sharing my faith with two people sitting next to me. All of a sudden, I felt someone in the seat behind me poke my elbow. The man said, "I see you are one of them." I said, "One of what?" He said, "One of those born-again Christians. My parents are born-again, but I'm an atheist." (Psalm 14 and Psalm 53) I said, "The fool says in his heart there is no God. All nature declares that God is so you are without an excuse." He said, "There is an empty seat next to me. Why don't you come, sit here, and tell me about God?" I said, "You have already made up your mind that God doesn't exist. I can't convince you that He exists. I will pray for you, in Jesus Name, that God Himself will reveal Himself to you in such a way that you will no longer be able to deny His existence anymore. Do it Lord. Amen. I said," God will reveal Himself to you now, don't worry." Then I went on to share Jesus with the people I was originally speaking with and led them to the Lord. The devil wanted to use the atheist to stop me from witnessing to the other two people. I didn't fall for it.

Airplanes are a good place to share the Gospel with people. They can't run. They can't hide. They can't get away. Holy Spirit can lead you into when to witness and when not to witness. He knows whose hearts are open and whose hearts are closed. Just obey Him in every situation.

There are many gifts of the Holy Spirit. I cannot possibly list them all or mention them all in this book. Even in the Old Testament, people had the Holy Spirit giftings.

Judges 13:24-25 "And the Spirit of the Lord began to move him, (Samson) ,at times in the camp of Dan. Judges Chapters 14 and 16 tell of the life of Samson. He had super-human strength that could slay his enemies, carry away the gates of the city, knock down thick pillars, made of stone, and bring down the entire house where the Philistines had gathered to worship their false god, Dagon.

Today we have a group of very strong men known as , "The Power Team." They do many feats of physical strength while witnessing how Jesus Christ changed their lives. God gave them supernatural strength to rip thick phone books in pieces, bend iron rods in half, and do many other feats to the Glory of God.

People tell the Bible Story of David and Goliath. They forget that in 1 Samuel 16:13, Samuel anointed David with oil and the Spirit of the Lord, (Holy Spirit), came upon David from that time forward. Later on, David was the only one not afraid of the giant, Goliath. He stood against the giant with the Power of God operating in him and through him. He slew the giant and cut off his head. The Spirit of the Lord gave David boldness, fearlessness, and total Victory. He can do the same for us.

While in Uganda, two men approached me and told me about two other men claiming to be the prophets at the Wailing Wall in Revelation 11:3-13. These two prophets were lying because the prophets at the Wailing Wall are not here on earth walking around yet. They are sent down to earth, by God to prophesy a thousand two hundred and three score days clothed in sack cloth..

In Revelation 11:4 it says ,"These are the two olive trees, and the two candlesticks standing before the God of the earth." They are clearly mentioned again in Zechariah Chapter 4:12-14. They are the two olive branches - the two anointed ones, that stand by the Lord of the whole earth."They are in heaven right now. I believe they are responsible for pouring fresh oil through the golden pipes out of themselves . In verse 2, we see a candlestick with a bowl and seven lamps and seven pipes to the seven lamps are on top of it. In verse 6, it says, "Not by might, nor by power, but by my spirit, says the Lord of hosts.

I believe they are pouring oil into the seven churches listed in Revelation 2 and 3, as the Lord directs them. They are not here on earth yet. These two anointed ones are sent to earth, by the Wailing Wall, after the church (Body of Christ) is already raptured in Revelation 7. The Body of Christ is up in heaven, so these olive trees (anointed ones), are no longer needed to pour the oil into the seven churches. Their new assignment is to prophesy by the Wailing Wall.

If I hadn't read my Bible, I may have believed these false prophets and been deceived by them. I knew right away that they were false, lying prophets.

If we look at the Ascension of Jesus Christ, in Acts Chapter 1, the two men in white apparel (angels) said, "This same Jesus which is taken up from you into heaven shall so come in like manner as you have seen him go into heaven." This same Jesus will return in the sky. He is not walking around in a physical body now. Anyone walking around claiming to be Jesus Christ , is a liar and a false Christ.

Matthew 24:23 Jesus said, "Then if any man shall say unto you, Lo, here is Christ, or there; believe it not. For there shall arise false Christs, and false prophets, and shall show great signs and wonders." In verse 27, Jesus said , "For as the lightning comes out of the east, and shines even unto the west, so shall also the coming of the Son of Man be." He is coming in the sky.

We are living in a time when lies, deceptions, and half-truths seem to be everywhere. Unless we study God's Holy Bible, we will not know what God says is right from what God says is wrong. We will think that the evil promoted by the lying media, is good and the truth of God's Word, is evil. Your moral compass will be amoral or totally immoral, if your value system is the world's value system. The devil's people call evil good and good, evil. Anyone telling the Truth of God's Word is called a hater. Truth is Not Relative. There are Eternal Truths that are True Forever and Do Not Change. God is Truth. His Word is Truth. God is the author of all truth now and for all eternity. Anything contrary to God's Word, is a Satanic Lie. Read the Bible and be set free from Satan's Lies.

Isaiah 5:20-24, "Woe unto them that call evil good, and good evil; that put darkness for light, and light for darkness; that put bitter for sweet, and sweet for bitter! Woe unto them that are mighty to drink wine, and men of strong drink, which justify the wicked for reward, (take bribes), and take away the righteousness of the righteous from him! Therefore as the fire devours the stubble, and the flame consumes the chaff, so their root shall be rottenness, and their blossom shall go up as dust: because they have cast away the law of the Lord of hosts, and despised the word of the Holy One of Israel."

Isaiah 28:7-8 "But they also have erred through wine, and through strong drink they are out of the way; the priest and the prophet have erred through strong drink, they are swallowed up of wine, they are out of the way (God's Way) through strong drink; they err in vision, they stumble in judgment."

Sadly, many pastors, ministers, elders, priests, prophets, and leaders have left God's Word behind and have embraced a "user friendly" attitude that condones all the world's wickedness. They refuse to preach anything that will be contrary to "public opinion" even when "public opinion" is in direct opposition to God and His Holy Bible. God will hold them accountable for not preaching the truth of His Word. If the Bible offends anyone, their heart is not right with God. They are in sin and need to repent and put the sin out of their lives.

These preachers who only preach the " love of God" and refuse to preach the "judgment of God on the wicked", are helping to populate hell, instead of heaven. God will hold them accountable for the souls they are destroying because they refuse to preach the entire Bible. May God raise up real pastors who love God and love souls enough to feed His Sheep the Whole Truth of God's Word.

Read the Bible for yourself. Make sure you understand God's Position on the issues of life. Jesus Creates babies in the womb of their mother's. The fruit of the womb is Jesus's reward. Jeremiah 1:4, Psalm 139:13-19 KJB and many other scriptures show that a baby is a precious gift from God and He creates every child for a Divine Purpose. People were never monkeys and monkeys were never people. Darwin's lie of Evolution is not a science, but an "Anti-God, Anti-Christ Religious Theory of Atheism. It is man's attempt to explain how he came to exist, without believing in a Divine Creator. God calls these people Fools in Psalm 14. It is sad that Stephen Hawkins was deceived by Satan and was used to deceive other people. All I can do is pray for people that the lie of evolution will be broken off of them and they will know Jesus.

> In Matthew Chapter 4, Jesus was tempted by Satan. Every time, Jesus answered Satan with, "It is Written." Jesus quoted the scriptures and had Victory over the devil. We must do the same.

> In Ephesians Chapter 6:17, the Bible says, "And take the helmet of Salvation, and the sword of the Spirit (Holy Spirit), which is the Word of God." If you don't study the Word of God, you have no sword to defend yourself against the devil.

> Hebrews 4:12 "For the Word of God is quick, and powerful, and sharper than any two edged sword, piercing even to the dividing asunder of soul and spirit, and of the joints and marrow; and is a discerner of the thoughts and intents of the heart."

The Word of God is the mirror we should be reading and looking at, to see if we are really lined up with God and what He says is right. There is a lot more to Christianity then just saying, "I am a Christian." A Christian is supposed to be a Christ Follower every day of the week. If you don't read your Bible and know what Jesus says is right, how can you really live for Him and follow Him? Statistics show that over 65% of Christians do not read their Bibles and very few can even list the Ten Commandments. I believe the percentage is higher than 65%.

> Ephesians 4:21-23, "The truth is in Jesus. That you put off the old man, which is corrupt according to deceitful lusts; And be renewed in the spirit of your mind; And that you put on the new man, which after God is created in righteousness and true holiness." As we see here, people need to renew their minds with the Word of God. The old, demonic mindsets, old attitudes, old lusts, old wicked ideas, have to go. Everything the devil has planted in our minds

has to go. If we read God's Word, we will replace the devil's lies, deceptions, and half-truths, with God's Eternal Truths. A person who doesn't read and study God's Word, stays a spiritual baby and never grows up to stand in the Authority and Power God has given them against the devil. They won't ever be able to fulfill the call of God on their lives.

Sadly, there are many spiritual babies that have known Jesus for years, sitting in the pews, doing nothing to advance the Kingdom of God, on planet earth. They won't read God's Word, they won't obey the Holy Spirit, they won't renew their minds with the Word of God, they won't deny themselves and follow Jesus, and they will never fulfill the call of God on their lives. Don't let this be you. Give Your entire heart and life to Jesus. Read the Bible. There are over 8,800 promises that God has for you, if you obey Him. There is a huge plan and purpose for your life. You will only fulfill it if you totally surrender your life to the Will of God.

> John 14:26 Jesus said, "But the Comforter, which is the Holy Ghost, whom the Father will send in my name, he shall teach you all things, and bring all things to your remembrance, whatsoever I have said unto you."

If you don't read the Bible and get God's Truth into your mind and heart, you will be deceived by the lies and twistedness of the devil. He operates through deceived people, the media, Hollywood, politicians, false pastors, evolutionists, false ideologies, etc...If you don't read the Word of God, you will not be able to discern right from wrong and good from evil.

For example, if you don't read Deuteronomy 18: 9-12, you will buy your children witchcraft books, wizard tapes and movies, Ouija boards, dungeon and dragon games, tarot cards, etc... not realizing that those who practice these things are an Abomination to God. A witch, a wizard, a necromancer (someone who contacts spirits of the dead), enchanters, spell casters, divination, etc.. are all abominations to God.

Sadly, I have seen the demonic books for sale at Church rummage sales. Much of the Body of Christ has been deceived and compromised by the devil, Hollywood and popular opinion.

There is No Such Thing As A Good Witch. Their spiritual power comes from Satan, and not God. Anyone operating in spiritual power that is not Holy Spirit's Power, is serving Satan and not God. The earth gives no power at all. There are only two sources of spiritual power, God's Power and Satan's Power. Satan is a fallen angel and his power is limited. God is the Creator of Everything Seen and Unseen and His Power is Unlimited.

Hosea 4:6 "My people are destroyed for lack of knowledge." If you continue reading, God's people have lost their reverence for God. They have fallen into sin, complacency, wickedness, and whoredoms.

Don't let the devil destroy you or your family members. Read God's Word, press into the Lord Jesus, surrender your entire life to Jesus and be led by the Spirit of God into Father God's Will for your life. Believe God! Believe God's Truths! Fill your heart, mind and life with the Living Word of God that is able to Save, Deliver and Heal You. Know the Truth and Be Set Free. God's Word is Truth.

CHAPTER 10

THE PARABLE OF THE TEN VIRGINS AND THE LORD

Matthew 25: 1-27 "Then Shall the Kingdom of Heaven be likened unto ten virgins, which took their lamps, and went forth to meet the bridegroom. And five of them were wise, and five were foolish."

I asked the Lord to show me what made the wise, wise and what made the foolish, foolish? He immediately led me to Proverbs chapter 1 verses 20-32. "Wisdom cries without; she utters her voice in the streets: she cries in the chief place of concourse in the openings of the gates: in the city, she utters her words saying, ' how long, you simple ones, will you love simplicity? And the scorners delight in their scorning, and fools hate knowledge?'" We see here that fools, like the foolish virgins, hated knowledge.

Verse 23 "Turn you at my reproof: behold, I will pour out my spirit unto you, I will make known my words unto you."

If we look at Proverbs 2:6 " For the Lord gives wisdom: out of his mouth comes knowledge and understanding." The Lord is pleading with people to receive reproof-correction. He has given us His Spirit and His Word – the Holy Bible.

Proverbs 1:24 " Because I have called and you refused, I have stretched out my hand and no man regards; But you have set at naught all my counsel, and would none of my reproof; I also will laugh at your calamity; I will mock when your fear comes as desolation and your destruction comes as a whirlwind, when distress and anguish come upon you."

Verse 29, " For they hated knowledge, and did not choose the fear of the Lord; they would none of my council: they despised my reproof, Therefore shall they eat of the fruit of their own way, and be filled with their own devices."

We see here that fools hate knowledge. They refuse to be corrected. They refuse God's attempt to correct them with His Word and His Spirit. They refuse to fear God and depart from evil. They are the foolish virgins.

Back to Matthew 25:3 "They that were foolish took their lamps, and took no oil with them; but the wise took oil in their vessels with their lamps."

Oil is symbolic of the Holy Spirit of God. In 1 Samuel 16:13 "Then Samuel took the Horn of oil, and anointed David in the midst of his brethren: and the Spirit of the Lord Came Upon David from that day forward." Holy Spirit was upon David, enabling him to fight and slay Goliath.

Back to Matthew 25:3 The foolish took no oil. If you have a lamp, but no oil, you are in darkness. Without the oil, the lamp cannot be lit.

In Matthew chapter 5:14 Jesus said, " You are the light of the world. A city that is set on a hill cannot be hid." Verse16 " Let your light so shine before men, that they may see your good works, and glorify your Father which is in heaven."

The foolish virgins had no light. They were not shining for Jesus. Their lamps had gone out. They were in darkness, doing works of darkness.

In Matthew 25:9-11 The foolish virgins were not ready when the bridegroom, Jesus, came. They had resisted God's Word, God's Spirit and God's reproof and correction. They refused to obey God and put the sin out of their lives. The wise who were ready went inside with Jesus and the door was shut. The foolish ones were locked outside. They said, "Lord, Lord open to us." Jesus said, " Verily I say unto you, I know you not." Because they denied Jesus in how they were living their lives, He denied knowing them. They couldn't enter heaven.

Titus 1:16 " They profess that they know God: but in works they deny him, being abominable, and disobedient, and unto every good work reprobate."

Matthew 10:33 Jesus said, " But whosoever shall deny me before men, him will I also deny before my Father which is in heaven." We can deny Jesus by living wicked, evil, lives. We deny him by refusing to let His Word and His Spirit work in us to prepare us for His return. Don't be a foolish virgin.

Here is a revelation, from God's Book of Revelation that the Holy Spirit showed me. It is my prayer that you will take heed, put sin out of your life, repent, let God's Word and God's Spirit change you to be more like Jesus and be ready for His return.

In Revelation chapter 20:15 "And whosoever was not written in the Book of Life was cast into the Lake of Fire." This speaks of those who rejected Jesus, and died in their sins, and are cast into the lake of fire at the Great White Throne of Judgement. They are gone forever. They are tormented in the lake of fire forever..

In Revelation chapter 22: 14-15 " Blessed are they that do his commandments, that they may have the right to the tree of life, and may enter into the gates into the city. For without are dogs, and sorcerers, and whoremongers, and murderers, and adulterers and whosoever lovers and makes a lie."

Who are these people who are locked outside of the gate to the New Jerusalem? They cannot enter in, just as the foolish virgins of Matthew 25 couldn't enter in. These are the disobedient, rebellious, stubborn, self-willed, Christians. They accepted Jesus into their hearts or they would have been thrown unto the Lake of Fire; But, they refused to let God's Word and God's Holy Spirit correct them. They continued embracing worldly things that displeased and dishonored Jesus.

John 14:23-24 Jesus said. " If a man loves me, he will keep my words: and my Father will love him, and we will come unto him and make our abode with him. He that loves me not keeps not my sayings: and the word which you hear is not mine, but the Father's which sent me."

Repent and Obey God's Bible and God's Holy Spirit. Put any and all sin out of your life. Live a life of Holiness so you can see God, enter the gates of New Jerusalem, and be with Jesus forever..

Honor the Lord with every thought, word, and deed. Allow Holy Spirit to change you, to work in you, to make you like Jesus. Stop watching wicked movies, soap operas, etc.... stop listening to lustful demonic music ... Stop fornicating... Stop the adultery... Stop watching the lying media. Read the Bible. Ask Holy Spirit to come and teach you God's truth from His Word. Get real and get right with God. Repent of anything offensive to God that you may have been watching, listening to, reading, etc.... Read the Bible. Know what God says about abortion, lust, adultery, fornication, gayness, transgender, streaking, lies, etc.... stop listening to public opinions, lying Hollywood, Peer pressure, magazines, etc.... and get God's wisdom, God's truth, and God's Understanding. Fear God (Reverence Him) and depart from evil. Otherwise, you will be a foolish virgin who spends all eternity locked outside gnashing your teeth and regretting your wicked life. You will watch others enter unto Heaven-God's presence, God's beauty, God's throne room... while you are locked outside forever with nothing to show for your life but disgrace? Be Wise, Not Foolish.

SANCTIFICATION

The word "sanctify" means to make holy, to set apart as holy, to make free from sin, to make productive of spiritual blessing…

God's word speaks of sanctification as follows: John 17:17 Jesus prayed, " sanctify them through your truth; your word is truth."

1 Corinthians 1:30-31 "But of God you are in Christ Jesus, who of God is made unto us wisdom, and righteousness, and sanctification, redemption; that, he that glories; let him glory in the Lord."

Ephesians 5:25-26 "Husbands, love your wives, even as Christ also loved the church and gave himself for it: that he might sanctify and cleanse it with the washing of water by the word." Here we see that the word of God sanctifies and cleanses God's people.

Hebrews 13:12 "Wherefore Jesus also, that he might sanctify the people with his own blood, suffered outside the gate."

1 Peter 1:1-2 Peter, an apostle of Jesus Christ, to the strangers scattered throughout Pontus, Galatia, Cappadocia, Asia, and Bithynia, elect according to the foreknowledge of God the Father, through Sanctification of the Holy Spirit, unto obedience and sprinkling of the blood of Jesus Christ: Grace unto you and peace be multiplied. Notice here that Holy Spirit sanctified people into obedience to Christ.

1 Corinthians 1:2-3 "Unto the Church of God, which is at Corinth, to them that are sanctified in Christ Jesus, called to be Saints, with all that in every place call upon the name of Jesus Christ Our Lord, both theirs and ours. Grace be unto you, and peace from God our Father, and from the Lord Jesus Christ."

A saint is a person who has repented of their sins and has received Jesus Christ into their heart and life. No church can make anyone a saint. Their personal relationship with Christ, will determine whether they are " Sanctified in Christ," or not.

1 Corinthians 6:9-11 " Don't you know that the unrighteous shall not inherit the kingdom of God? Don't be deceived: neither fornicators, nor idolaters, nor adulterers, nor effeminate, nor abusers of themselves with mankind, nor thieves, nor covetous, nor drunkards, nor revilers, nor extortioners, shall inherit the kingdom of God, And such were some of you: but you are washed, but you are sanctified, but you are justified in the name of the Lord Jesus and by the Spirit of our God." This is how they were, at one time, but God is changing their hearts and lives through faith in Jesus and by Holy Spirit.

1 Thessalonians 4:3-5 " For this is the will of God, even your sanctification that you should abstain from fornication. That every one of you should know how to possess his vessel in sanctification and honor; not in the lust of concupiscence,

even as gentiles which know not God." To be sanctified, sexual purity is very important. Fornication (sex outside of marriage) is a sin, along with adultery, sodomy, gayness, transgender, watching pornography, beast ology, cross-dressing, and other sexual perversions etc.

If we want to be ready for Jesus Christ's return, we must walk closely with Him, allow His Word to transform us by the renewing our minds, allow His Holy Spirit to teach us, convict us and rid us of anything not pleasing to God and stop any and all sexual sin and lust. We must walk with Jesus, believe in Him, and love Him enough to want to please Him by being sexually pure..

> 1 Corinthians 6:15-20 "Know you not that your bodies are the members of Christ? Shall I then take the members of Christ, and make them members of a harlot? God forbid, What? Don't you know that he which is joined to a harlot is one body? For two, he says, shall be one flesh. But he that is joined to the Lord is one Spirit. Flee fornication. Everything that a man does is without the body; but he that commits fornication sins against his own body. What? Don't you know your body is the Temple of the Holy Ghost which is in you, which you have of God, and you are not your own? For You Are bought with a price (. The precious blood of Jesus Christ). Therefore glorify God in your body and in your spirit which are God's."

We must allow God's Word and God's Holy Spirit and the Blood of Jesus to sanctify and cleanse us, in order to be a wise virgin, ready to go with Christ. Sexual sin will keep us from being with Christ. Sexual sin will keep us from being Sanctified and ready. We must put it away from us, with all diligence. Repent of any sexual sin or other types of sin in your life. Stop it now! Read God's Word and allow his Word to work in your heart and life. Listen to the conviction of God's Holy Spirit and repent.

Is he showing you any sin in your life, and wrong attitudes, any wrong mindsets, wrong actions... Repent speedily. The Holy Spirit teaches us, guides us, corrects us, and prepares us for Jesus Christ's return. As we read God's Holy Bible, the Holy Spirit quickens God's Words deep into our hearts and Spirits. He guides us, directs us, and helps us to avoid the devil's traps; and to really live for Christ. We must be the wise virgins, not the foolish ones in Matthew 25: 1-13.

> Hebrews 12:14 "Follow peace with all men, and Holiness, without which no man shall see the Lord." We must walk in Holiness, not worldliness.

> Romans 8:1-2 "There is, therefore, no condemnation to them which are in Christ Jesus, who walk not after the flesh, but after the Spirit. For The law of the spirit of life in Jesus Christ has made me free from the law of sin and death."

If you follow Holy Spirit, you will not sin against God. If you revert back to the flesh, you are guaranteed to sin. The flesh profits nothing. The Holy Spirit is life, and light, and Truth.

If we read Galatians 5: 16-21 It lists the works of the flesh that profit nothing but misery. Verse 16 "Walk in the Spirit (Holy Ghost), and you shall not fulfill the lust of the flesh. For the flesh lusts against the Spirit, and the Spirit against the flesh: and these are contrary the one to the other: so that you cannot do the things that you would. But if you be led of the Holy Spirit, you are not under the law (legalism)."

> Verse 19 " Now the works of the flesh are manifest, which are these, adultery, fornication, uncleanness, lasciviousness, idolatry, witchcraft, hatred, variance, emulations, wrath, strife, seditions, heresies, envying's, murders, drunkenness, raveling's, and such like: of the which I told you before, as I have also told you in time past, that they which do such things shall not inherit the kingdom of God.

> Galatians 5: 22-26 "But the fruit of the Spirit is love, joy, peace, long-suffering, gentleness, goodness, faith, meekness, temperance: against such there is no law. And they that are Christ's have crucified the flesh with the affections and lusts. If we live in the Spirit let us walk in the Spirit. Let us not be desirous of vain glory, provoking one another, envying one another."

Galatians 6:14 " But God forbid that I should glory, save in the cross of our Lord Jesus Christ, by whom the world is crucified unto me, and I unto the world."

1 John 2:15-17 " Love not the world, neither the things that are in the world. If any man loves the world, the love of the Father is not in him. For all that is in the world, the lust of the flesh, and the lust of the eyes, and the pride of life, is not of the Father but is of the world. And the world passes away and the lust thereof: but he that does the will of God abides forever."

Matthew 6:19-21 "Lay not up for yourselves treasures upon earth, where moth and rust doth corrupt, and where thieves break in and steal: but lay up for yourselves treasures in Heaven where neither moth nor rust doth corrupt and where thieves do not break through nor steal: for where your treasure is there will your heart be also."

Matthew 6:24 "No man can serve two masters: for either he will hate the one and love the other; or else he will hold to the one, and despise the other. Ye cannot serve God and Mammon.

Mammon - riches - That which is made secure or deposited . Riches as regarded as an object of worship and greedily pursued, wealth or material gain as an evil, more or less deified. Deified- made as one's God.

1 Timothy 6:6-10 "But Godliness with contentment is great gain: For we brought nothing into the world, and it is certain we can carry nothing out. And having food and raiment let us be there with content. But they that will be rich fall into temptation and a snare, and into many foolish and hurtful lusts which drown men in destruction and perdition. For the Love of Money is the root of all evil: which while some coveted after, they have erred from the faith, and pierced themselves through with many sorrows."

People who love money are capable of murder, lying, taking bribes, stealing, perjury, and every other wickedness imaginable. They sell drugs, do sex trafficking of innocent children, engage in all kinds of perversion and wickedness, to get money. Some rock bands have sold their souls to Satan for fame, fortune, wealth and popularity.

Mark 8: 36-37 " For what shall it profit a man if he shall gain the whole world, and lose his own soul? Or what shall a man give in exchange for his soul?"

Malachi 3:8-12 "Will a man rob God? Yet ye have robbed me. But you say, wherein have we robbed Thee? In tithes and offerings. You are cursed with a curse: for ye have robbed me, even this whole nation. Bring ye all the tithes into the storehouse that there may be meat in mine house, and prove me now herewith, saith the Lord of hosts, if I will not open you the windows of heaven, and pour you out a blessing, that there shall not be room enough to receive it. And I will rebuke the Devourer for your sakes, and he shall not destroy the fruits of your ground; neither shall your vine cast her fruit before the time in the field, saith the Lord of hosts. "

To advance God's Kingdom on earth, funds are needed for Ministries. God is testing you to see if you will give at least one tenth of what he has blessed you with , to advance the gospel on planet Earth. Do You Love Money More Than Jesus? Are you robbing God? Everything really belongs to him anyway.

This life is temporary, your soul is eternal. Your soul and spirit will live on, either in heaven or hell. To exchange your Eternal Soul for temporary riches, lust, fame or Fortune is a horrible trade-off, that has forever consequences. Forever is many lifetimes. It never ends. This life on earth is temporary.

Parents spend time and money preparing their children for college or a great job, in the future, but they neglect to bring them to Jesus, for eternal life in heaven. Eternity is more important than this temporary life we have now. Parents neglect to take their children to Sunday school, Vacation Bible School, read them children's Bible stories, share Biblical truths with them, etc....

Sadly many parents have believed the atheist lie of evolution and do not realize that they, themselves, are unique special creations of Almighty God, who loves them. They and their children are precious to God, who created them, in the womb, for his Divine Purpose for their lives. Jesus wants a love relationship with you and your children and future generations. You are so precious to God that he (Jesus) came to earth in human form to die for your sins so you could be washed clean, forgiven, and go to heaven. He paid for your sins and mine with his holy, sinless, blood. He rose from the dead on the third day and was seen by over 500 people. He is now in heaven seated at the right side of Father God, interceding for you, because he loves you. Jesus prays for you.

If you want Jesus to be your personal Savior and Lord, welcome him into your heart and life. Ask his forgiveness for your sins and ask him to save you, wash you clean and help you to live for him. He is only a prayer away.

> Romans 10:9-10 "That if you will confess with your mouth the Lord Jesus, and shalt believe in your heart that God has raised him from the dead, you shall be saved. For with the heart man believeth unto righteousness; and with the mouth confession is made unto salvation." Believe his blood was shed for you personally. Believe he rose from the dead and ascended into heaven. Accept Jesus into your heart and life and tell someone you did it. Confess Jesus as your Savior and Lord today. Life is short. No one knows if they have tomorrow.

Read the Gospels starting in John. Then read Matthew, Mark, and Luke. Get to really know Jesus. See what Jesus said, what Jesus taught, what miracles Jesus did, how Jesus healed the sick, preached heaven and hell, raised the dead, delivered people tormented by demons, etc... The miracles Jesus did, the believers in Christ can do also, by the Power of Holy Spirit. Come to Jesus today and live for Him every day.

> Psalm 91:4-7 , we can say, "It is written, no pestilence will come near my dwelling place. Verse 10 "There shall be no evil befall me, neither shall any plague come near my dwelling. For He shall give His angels charge over me, to keep me in all my ways."
> We can speak these scriptures over our bodies every day.

A few times I have gotten stuck in my car on the road, whether a flat tire, a fan belt snap or another issue. The Lord has always sent someone to help me, when I asked Him for help. Sometimes I didn't know if it was a human or an angel that helped me.

In 1984, my son, my daughter, and I were on our way to a church across the river to be "believer baptized in water", when my fan belt snapped. I was stranded in a 7-11 parking lot. I put my hood up and prayed to the Lord for help. Immediately a car pulled up. A man came over ,looked under the hood, and said ,"Your fan belt has snapped. Then he said, "I can help you. It will take about 20 minutes to get you a fan belt, return, and put it on for you. He drove off, came back with a fan belt and fixed my car. (There were no repair shops or car parts places open on Sundays back in 1984.) He refused any money for labor. We left, got to Church on time, and were Believer Baptized, in water, that day. Whether the person was a human being or an angel, I don't know, but his timing was perfect.

Even before I really knew Jesus in my heart, God was watching over me. I believed there was a God, but I really didn't have a relationship with him yet, at the time of the following incident. Around 1980, we were trying to buy a house. The lawyer phoned and said that one paper that had to be signed by the V.A. office down the city had not been signed. He said, our closing would be delayed because of that one piece of paper. I said, what if I go down to the V.A. office, have them sign the paper and bring it with me to the closing can we have the closing?" I didn't want to delay because interest rates were expected to go up. He agreed that it would work.

I phoned my husband who was working down the city at the time, took our two children onto the train platform to catch a train, and waited for the train to arrive. One child was in an umbrella stroller. The other one I had by the hand. A man came onto the platform and began to steal the pay telephone. He was cutting the phone wire with a knife. After he had the phone in one hand and the knife in the other, he began to take a step toward us. I prayed, "God help me." Right at that moment, another man came up the stairs onto the platform. The man with the knife looked at him and looked at me and ran down the stairs. Whether or not it was a man or an angel that showed up just in the nick of time, I don't know. His timing was perfect. If he had been a few minutes later, either the man with the knife or I, would have been dead. I would have fought him to the death to protect my children.

Have there been times in your life that you were in danger, and God helped you? Maybe you didn't realize it was God who sent someone when you needed them. Maybe God gave you wisdom as to what to do when your car went into a skid. Maybe you overcame all odds and had victory over cancer. It just disappeared. Miracles happen every day.

Every morning before we get out of bed, Paul and I pray for our family members, friends, brethren and ourselves. We pray for angels of protection to surround any vehicles we ride in, ride on, or drive, fly in, or sail on and keep us safe from any accidents, incidents, evil or harm, in Jesus Name. Amen! We also say, "In the Name of Jesus we decree that any plans, devices, schemes, or plots of the devil or any of his agents against us are null, void, of no effect, and cannot manifest, in Jesus Name. Amen! It is important to dismantle the enemy before he can do anything against us.

One time my son-in-law bought tires for their car from a dealer who put them on the vehicle. My son-in-law, daughter, and grandchildren were in the car, on the highway going 65 miles per hour, when my son-in-law realized something was wrong. He pulled over and was shocked to find that none of the lugs had been tightened on the tires. One lug had broken off one tire and they could have all been killed. He tightened all the lugs. Any of those tires could have flown off the vehicle at any time. They could have killed my family members and other drivers who would have tried to dodge the flying tires. God and His Angels protected them.

We need to realize that angels were not created in the image of God. Human beings were. We, the believers in Christ, are joint heirs with Christ. The angels are not. In Revelation 1:6 and Revelation 5:10, the Bible says we, the believers in Christ, are kings and priests to our God. We are part of God's Family. Jesus died on the cross to save us. He did not die on the cross to save the fallen angels. He died on the cross to save fallen people. Angels are not over us. We are over them. They were created to help us.

Satan is a fallen angel. The believers in Christ, who have been Baptized in the Holy Spirit (Holy Ghost), have Jesus's Authority and Holy Ghost Power to rebuke Satan and command him to leave, in Jesus Name. Satan must bow to Jesus. Jesus is God. Satan is a created being- just a fallen angel. He is not God. He will never be God.

People who do not have Jesus in their heart and life, do not have Father God, or the Holy Spirit. They have no power at all against Satan, his wicked attacks, and his wicked lusts, alcoholism, drug addictions, etc...In their flesh, without God, they cannot overcome the devil who is the enemy of their souls. Satan wants to steal, kill, and destroy as many people as he can, because he knows his time is short. Jesus came to give us life more abundantly. Trust Jesus Today. Give Him your heart and life. He Loves You!

STATUE WORSHIP / IDOLATRY

Commandment 1, Thou shall have no other gods before me". Exodus 20:3

Leviticus 26:1 "You shall make no idols nor graven image, neither rear up a standing image, neither shall you set up any image of stone in your land, to bow down unto it. For I am the Lord your God."

Deuteronomy 4:15-19. "Take good heed unto yourselves; for you saw no manner of similitude on the day that the Lord spoke unto you in Horeb out of the midst of the fire. Lest you corrupt yourselves, and make you a graven image, the similitude of any figure, the likeness of male or female.. The likeness of any beast that is on the earth, the likeness of any winged fowl that flies in the air. The likeness of any thing that creeps on the ground, the likeness of any fish that is in the water beneath the earth: And lest you lift up your eyes unto heaven, and when you see the sun, and the moon, and the stars, even all the host of heaven, should be driven to worship them, and serve them, which the Lord thy God has divided unto all nations under the whole heaven."

Don't make golden, silver, wood and stone idols of people, animals, birds, fish etc...and worship them. They cannot see, hear, or answer your prayers. They are vanity and anger the God of Heaven. Don't worship the sun, moon and stars. Worship God, the Creator of all Heaven and Earth and everything seen and unseen.

CHAPTER 11
DO NOT WORSHIP PEOPLE OR ANGELS

The only one Jesus taught us to pray to is, "Our Father in Heaven." He never taught his disciples to pray to anyone else. It does not please God when we elevate any human being over Him. He deserves our time, our praise, our worship, our respect, our love, our thanks, and our awe (reverence). He is God Alone.

> John 16:23-24 Jesus said, "And in that day you shall ask me nothing. Whatsoever you shall ask the Father in my name, he will give it you. So far you have asked nothing in my name: ask, and you shall receive, that your joy may be full."

God doesn't promise to answer any prayers prayed to human beings. He promises to answer prayers prayed to the Father. Father is God. When Jesus taught the disciples to pray, he taught them to begin by saying, "Our Father." He never taught them to submit a prayer to anyone else.

> John14:13 Jesus said, "And whatsoever you shall ask in my name, that will I do; that the Father may be glorified in the Son. If you ask anything in my name, I will do it."

In 1984, I repented of my sins and asked Jesus to come into my heart and life and be my Savior and Lord. I believed he died on the cross for me and rose again. The men who led me to Jesus, told me to read the Bible beginning in the Gospel of John. When I got to John Chapter 14, I began praying that Father would heal my son's brain of mental retardation, in Jesus Name. I prayed all summer for my son. He had begun school in the retarded class and the teacher said, "I couldn't teach him anything all year."

When my son went back to school in September 1984, the teacher phoned my house and said, "Last year I couldn't teach your son anything. This year, his mind is like a sponge. He is learning at a fast rate. What happened?" I said, "Jesus is healing Brian's brain." She hesitated to say anything so I repeated myself and said, "Jesus is healing my son's brain." She said, "That's nice" and hung up. That year he caught up on kindergarten work and began first grade work. He tested out of the retarded program and was placed in the mild learning disability classroom for second and third grades. In fourth grade, he was placed in a behavior class on the honor roll. Fifth grade to eighth grade he went to Christian School on the honor roll. Grades nine to twelve, he went back to public school on the honor roll. He graduated from Dutchess Community College and Suny New Paltz on the Dean's List. He drives a car and has worked as an accountant for many years now. Nothing is Impossible for My Jesus.

In my prayer, for my son, I prayed that he would be able to read and understand the Word of God, in Jesus Name. My son began reading the adult King James Bible at age 7 and understood it. God is Faithful to answer our prayers.

> 1 John 5:14-15 "And this is the confidence that we have in him, that, if we ask anything according to his will he hears us: And if we know he hears us, whatsoever we ask, we know that we have the petitions that we desired of him." It is God's Will that everyone be able to read and understand His Word. If you have asked, keep asking until you receive your answers from Him. Don't ask once and forget it. Keep asking expecting to receive your petitions.

Sometimes people pray silly prayers out of immaturity and ignorance. For example, when I was a teenager, I dated a boy that my parents didn't like. I knew I had to break up with the boy. I prayed that I would die before morning. I'm glad that God didn't answer that prayer. I thank God for unanswered prayers.

Sometimes people pray prayers out of covetousness and greed and lust. He won't answer the prayers that are prayed out of greed, un-Godly lusts, lust of the flesh, lust of the eye, and the pride of life. To pray for a million dollars, a yacht, an expensive car, a mink coat, a mansion, etc. are very selfish prayers.

If you are asking for money for ministry purposes, to help other people, to spread the Word of God, to bless others with food, medicines and fresh drinking water etc... the Lord will hear and answer those prayers. If you have a genuine need for food, money to pay your bills, money to clothe your children, etc... The Lord will hear you and help you. Many times He will cause someone to bless you with what you need.

There were times I needed funds for my Africa Mission trips. I would pray and ask the Lord to help me. No church sponsored me. Most of the trips to Africa were from our personal funds. The Lord put it on a sister in Christ's heart to hand me a check toward the mission trip. It was the exact amount I needed to travel to different villages and towns, for hotel rooms, and food for myself, my coordinator, and my interpreter.

Another time, my husband won a raffle and the money we needed came through that. The Lord always provided. Sometimes I would land back home with not even a dollar in my pocket. I had exactly, to the dollar, what I needed --no more and no less, for the Africa Mission Trip.

Sometimes people pray for sick relatives, sick brethren, and sick friends to be healed. Sometimes the Lord heals them here on earth; But other times He takes them to heaven. There are no sick people in heaven Everyone is well, happy and healthy, up there. They are not suffering with any more illnesses, blindness, pains, aches, etc... They are perfectly well and whole.

Some people get angry with God and walk away from God because He chose to heal their loved one by taking them to heaven, instead of healing them on earth. He did answer your prayer. Your loved one is healed.

God's Word makes it clear that we are not to worship angels. In Hebrews 1:13-14, "But to which of the angels did he say at any time, Sit on my right hand, until I make your enemies your footstool? Are they not all ministering spirits, sent forth to minister for them who shall be heirs of salvation?" Jesus was never an angel. He always was and is God. He sits at the right hand of God the Father, in heaven. He is worshipped by the angels, as God.

If we look back at Hebrews1:8, we see that Jesus is God's Son, the heir of all things. By Jesus, the world was made. Jesus is the brightness of God's glory and the image of God's person who upholds all things by His power. When he purged our sins, he sat down at the right hand of Father and is worshipped by all the saints and angels, in heaven.

Hebrews1:7-8 "And of the angels he said, Who makes his angels spirits and his ministers a flame of fire, But unto the Son he said, "Thy throne, O God, is for ever and ever; a scepter of righteousness is the scepter of your kingdom."

Jesus is God. He created the angels. He rolled out the heavens as a scroll and hung the earth on nothing. He set the boundaries of the seas, He tells the birds when to migrate, He tells the leaves when to change color and fall from the trees, the orbits of the planets are set by Him, the paths for the lightnings are set by Him, and all nature declares that He Is, so atheists have no excuse.

In Hebrews 13: 2 "Be not forgetful to entertain strangers; for thereby some have entertained angels unawares." Angels can look like humans at times. There are different types of angels that were created by God for different types of missions. Angels do not look like little dolls, with wings, flying around singing popular songs.

Sometimes they appear in white, shining robes, as in the garden tomb. Other times they appear as men like in Acts 1:10-11. At times they hold back the winds of heaven and appear in might and power.

Colossians 2:18 "Let no man beguile you of your reward in a voluntary humility and worshipping of angels, intruding into those things which he has not seen, vainly puffed up in his fleshly mind." We are not to worship angels.

Revelation 22:8-9 "And I John saw these things, and heard them. And when I heard and seen, I fell down to worship before the feet of the angel which showed me these things. Then he said to me, "See you do it not, for I am thy fellow servant, and of thy brethren the prophets, and of them which keep the saying of this book: worship God." We are not to worship angels or human beings.

Beware of the new age movement "angel workshops," "angel worship", "seeking angels" etc... We are to seek God Himself.

Psalm 103:20 "Bless the Lord, you his angels, that excel in strength, that do his commandments, hearkening unto the voice of his word." Notice here that God's angels are continually listening for God's Word to be spoken so they can go into action. When we say, "It is written, and speak the Word of God, we release God's angels to carry out His Word and help us. If we speak negative words, we are releasing the devil's fallen angels to attack us and bring us more misery. We must be careful to release only what God's Word says, in Faith.

The Bible says in Proverbs 18:21 "Death and life are in the power of the tongue: and they that love it shall eat the fruit thereof." We can speak words of life or death into our situations. We will have what we speak into existence. If we speak words of doubt, unbelief, discouragement, fear, etc... we actually are releasing the devil's fallen angels to continue the misery they are causing. IF we speak the Word of God, we are releasing the Power of God and the angels of God to help us.

Over the years, I have asked Father God to send angels to do things. For example, "Father, send your angels to push these rain clouds out of my neighborhood so our yards won't flood, in Jesus Name. Amen." I have watched clouds, high winds, and storms leave my area after asking Father to send angels to remove them. "Father send your angels to push this wind and turbulence away from this airplane so we can have a smooth flight, in Jesus Name. Amen." We saw what appeared to be see through walls, about 20 feet from our plane, holding back the storm, the wind, and the turbulence. We had a smooth flight.

We can always ask Father to send angels to help us. They are available to help, if we ask for them. After all, they are ministering spirits to us, the heirs of salvation. They stand by and listen for us to speak the Word of God.

CHAPTER 12
INSIGHT INTO THE BOOK OF ACTS AND BEYOND

The following are some facts and incites that people don't think about, when they read The Book of Acts. These are not the only insights, but these are some that Holy Spirit revealed to me, personally. Read the book of Acts for yourself and see what he will reveal to you, personally. There are always more things to learn from Holy Spirit as He reveals God's truths from His Word. He is the Spirit of Truth, our Teacher, our Comforter and Friend.

In Acts Chapter 1, Luke spoke about Jesus's resurrection, and the fact that his disciples saw him alive forty days until he was taken up to heaven. In versus 4-5 Jesus told them to wait for the promise of the Father – the Baptism with the Holy Ghost. In verse 8 Jesus said "But you shall receive power after that the Holy Ghost is come upon you; and you shall be Witnesses unto me both in Jerusalem and in all Judea and in Samaria, and unto the uttermost part of the earth." In verse 9, They saw Jesus go up and a cloud received him out of their sight.

In Acts chapter 2, on the day of Pentecost, the Holy Spirit As A Mighty Wind filled the house and tongues of fire sat on them. They were all filled with the Holy Ghost and began to speak with other tongues as the Spirit gave them utterance. Acts 2: 11 The people heard them speaking in all the languages of the nation's, the wonderful works of God.

In Acts 2:38 Peter said, "Repent and be baptized in the name of Jesus Christ for the remission of sins, and you shall receive the gift of the Holy Ghost. For the promise is unto you, and to your children and to all that are afar off, even as many as the Lord Our God shall call." Notice the baptism of the Holy Ghost is for all generations to experience. It is even for people far off in the future – us. The Power of the Holy Spirit did not stop. His power is still released to us today through the Holy Ghost Baptism.

In Acts 3, we read about a lame man who was born lame from his mother's womb. They carried him to the gate everyday to beg for money from people entering into the temple. He asked Peter and John for money. In verse 6, Peter said, "Silver and gold have I none; but such as I have give I you: in the name of Jesus Christ of Nazareth rise up and walk. And he took him by the right hand and lifted him up and immediately his feet and ankle bones received strength." And he leapt up, stood and walked."

Think about this, the man was unable to walk for years. The muscles and bones in his legs, hips, thighs, ankles, feet, were all weak and shriveled from lack of use. All of a sudden, his ankle bones received strength. It was a miracle. He lept up, stood, and walked. Against all odds, he was healed. God's power manifested through the Holy Spirit and the Name of Jesus. This was after the disciples were baptized with the Holy Ghost, not before.

In Acts 4, The disciples were threatened not to speak or teach in Jesus's Name. They prayed for more boldness to speak God's Word and for God's healing power signs and wonders to be done in Jesus Name. The place was shaken and they were all filled with the Holy Ghost again. The Holy Ghost can keep filling us with more of Himself. We can ask for more of the Holy Spirit (Luke 11:9-13). An unlimited portion of Holy Spirit is ours, if we ask.

In Acts 5, two people lied to the Holy Ghost and fell down dead. Acts 5:12 says, " And by the hands of the Apostle's were many signs and wonders wrought among the people; and they were all with one accord in Solomon's porch." Notice here, there was unity among them – not division.

In Acts 5: 14-15 Believers were added to their numbers, and the sick were brought into the streets on beds and couches that at least the shadow of Peter passing by might overshadow some of them. Even Peter's shadow had a Holy Ghost anointing to heal people.

Acts 5:16 A multitude of people came out of the cities bringing the sick folks and those vexed with unclean spirits: and they were healed. In verse 17 the high priest and his friends were angry, grabbed the disciples and put them in prison for healing people. Anytime God raises up a healing evangelist, they suffer persecution from " religious" pastors, reverends and ministers who get angry and jealous that they cannot do the Miracles. Instead of being happy that people are being healed and ministered to, they are jealous and vicious.

It is sad that such things happen, even in the real body of Christ. If you really love God's sheep, you will want them to be healed, delivered from unforgiveness and pains and hurts of the past. You will want them to be healed emotionally, spiritually, and physically and be able to fulfill God's call on their lives. They are not your sheep, they belong to God. Grow them. Feed them the Word of God. Feed God's Sheep. Feed God's Lambs. Feed His Sheep!

In Acts 5:19-23 "But The angel of the Lord by Night, opened the prison doors, and brought the disciples forth." The high priest called the council together and the senate of Israel and sent a message to the prison to bring the disciples to them. The officers couldn't find them, saying, "The prison truly we found shut with all safety, and the keepers were standing outside in front of the doors, but when we opened, we found no man inside." Even though there were guards in front of the prison doors, the angel was able to get them out right past the guards.

The disciples were found in the temple teaching the people in Jesus name. Peter said, "We ought to obey God rather than you." In verse 33, The high priest and the counsel wanted to slay them. A Pharisee named Gamaliel said, "Refrain from these men, and let them alone; for if this counsel or this work be of men, it will come to nothing; But if it be of God, you cannot overthrow it; lest you be found even to fight against God." They took them, beat them, threatened them and let them go. In verse 41, " they departed from the council, rejoicing that they were counted worthy to suffer shame for His name." Notice, the persecution didn't hinder, discourage, or stop them. In verse 42, they ceased not to teach and preach Jesus Christ.

> Matthew 5:11-12 "Blessed are you, when men revile you, and persecute you, and shall say all manner of evil against you falsely, for my sake. Rejoice, and be exceeding glad: for great is your reward in heaven: for so persecuted they the prophets which were before you."

> Hebrews 11: 32-38 "And what shall I say? For the time would fail me to tell of Gideon, Barak, Samson, Jephthah, David, Samuel, and the prophets who through faith subdued kingdoms, wrought righteousness, obtained promises, stopped the mouths of lions, quenched the violence of fire, escaped the edge of the sword, out of weakness were made strong, waxed valiant in fight, turned to flight the armies of the aliens, women received their dead raised to life again: and others were tortured not accepting deliverance, that they might obtain a better Resurrection: and others had trial of cruel mocking and scourging, yes, moreover, of bonds of imprisonment; They were stoned, they were sown asunder, were tempted, were slain with the sword: they wandered about in sheepskins and goat skins; being destitute, afflicted, tormented,(of whom the world was not worthy); they wandered in deserts, and in mountains, and in dens and caves of the earth."

As we can see, Christians are not wimps. They stand for their faith and are willing to die for the cause of the Gospel of Jesus Christ. Many are persecuted in China, Iran, Afghanistan, Cuba and other nations around the world today. Many are in prison. Many have been tortured and murdered by communist/socialist/Marxist/satanic dictators who do not want people to believe in Jesus Christ and have eternal life. They are agents of the devil who hate Christ, hate Father God, hate the Jews, hate the ten commandments, hate the Bible, and hate all Christians.

In America, we have seen the persecution of Christians for their Biblical Values and Beliefs by the wicked ACLU. The Bible makes it clear that gayness is an Abomination to God. (Romans Chapter 1). To be forced to make gay wedding cakes (if you are a baker), make gay flower arrangements for gay weddings (if you are a florist), and deny your faith to condone what God's Holy Bible says is wrong, would make a Christian a sinner.

We would be in violation of God's Word to condone, approve of, and help people to sin against God. Our Constitution says we have freedom of religion, yet our evil court system has allowed Christians to be sued for their faith, contrary to Amendment One of our Constitution. Why?

" Congress shall make no law respecting an establishment of religion, or prohibiting the free exercise thereof; or abridging the freedom of speech, or of the press, or the right of the people to assemble, and to petition the government for a redress of grievances."

If Congress can't prohibit the free exercise of religion or Christian speech, why has the Supreme Court been able to ? How can the Supreme Court make the "law of separation of church and state," put it into the books as law, and keep the Gospel of Jesus Christ from being shared, preached, and taught in our schools, our colleges, our work places, and in society in general, against our Constitution? The Court is not supposed to be able to make laws. The lie of "separation of church and state " needs to be thrown out.

It was put in by wicked, atheist, Supreme Court Judges along with taking God and prayer out of our schools, promoting the atheist lie of evolution, stopping Christian's Freedom of Speech, murdering 62 million babies through abortion, and the other evil decisions that they had no right or authority to make. The court system has no right to be making laws. They are just supposed to enforce what was passed through the House and Senate. Yet the court has tried cases they had no business trying and put their decisions in as laws, bypassing the House and Senate. This has to be taken off our law books. These things never passed the House and Senate. Roe v Wade was another wicked court decision that bypassed the House and Senate along with many other wicked decisions.

Back to Acts 8:3-4 Saul persecuted the believers in Christ, pulling them out of their homes and taking them to prison. Because of the persecution, the believers were scattered abroad and went everywhere preaching the word. Persecution didn't stop the gospel. The gospel went everywhere, despite the wicked attempts to stop it.

In Acts 9: 1-31, Saul was taking letters from the high priest to Damascus, to the synagogues, to get the believers in Christ, bind them and take them to Jerusalem to destroy them. In verse three, suddenly a light from Heaven shined around Saul. He fell to the earth, and heard a voice saying unto him, " Saul, Saul, why are you persecuting me?" Saul said, "Who are you, Lord?" And the Lord said, " I am Jesus whom you persecute; it is hard for you to kick against the pricks." Notice here, Jesus said Saul was persecuting Him. When someone attacks God's people, they attack God. Jesus didn't say, "Why are you persecuting my people?" He said, " Why are you persecuting me?" God takes it personal.

In Acts 9:7-14, we see that the men with Saul heard a voice, but saw no man. Saul arose from the earth but was blind and needed someone to lead him by the hand into Damascus. Saul was fasting and praying when a disciple named Ananias was sent by God to recover his sight. Ananias was afraid to go near Saul because he had heard of the persecution Saul had done to the believers. The Lord said, "Go your way: for Saul is a chosen vessel unto me, to bear my name before the Gentiles and kings and children of Israel: For I will show him how great things he must suffer for my names sake."

When King David committed adultery with Uriah's wife, Bathsheba, and sent Uriah into the front line of the battle to be killed, Nathan the prophet came to David to confront him. David wrote Psalm 51. He said to God in verse four, "Against you, you only, have I sinned, and done this evil in your sight." The sin was not really against Bathsheba and Uriah. The sin was against God, His Commandments and His Word. All sin is against God Himself. Just as, all persecution against Christian people is against Jesus Christ, Himself.

Saul, who had persecuted Christians, became a full believer in Jesus Christ, suffered many perils, and wrote many books of the New Testament, while in prison in Rome. Jesus changes hearts and lives. Saul, a religious Pharisee, became a new person, in Christ. Instead of persecuting believers, he became a believer and preached the Gospel of Jesus Christ to many people, as the disciple Paul.

> 2 Corinthians 11:23-27 lists what Paul endured for Christ's sake. He was beaten, in prison frequently, in peril of death often, stoned, shipwrecked three times, stuck out at sea, in perils of waters, in perils of heathen, in perils of false brethren, etc.... Yet he kept his faith in Christ, to the end.

> In II Timothy 4:7-8, Paul says, "I have fought a good fight, I have finished my course, I have kept the faith: Henceforth there is laid up for me a crown of righteousness, which the Lord, the righteous judge, shall give me at that day: and not to me only, but unto all them who love his appearing."

We must all run the race and finish well. All of the promises of Holy Spirit in Revelation chapters 2 and 3 are to "He that overcomes." There are no promises to those who backslide, quit, or walk away, or compromise. All of the promises are to those who overcome sin, lust, and the devil. To each and every church, the promises are to the overcomers. Holy Spirit gives direction and correction to some churches. Ephesus, Pergamos, Thyatira, Sardis, and the Laodicean Church. He encouraged the persecuted church, Smyrna, to be faithful even unto death. He opens doors of ministry to the Philadelphia Church because they keep His Word and don't deny His Name. He makes the fake Jews that are of the synagogue of Satan (which say they are Jews and are not, but lie) worship before the feet of the Philadelphia Church members and to know Christ loves us.

The Philadelphia Church represents those who know Jesus as their Savior and have surrendered their entire lives to Jesus as Lord. They are, " crucified with Christ."They are dead to selfishness, their own agendas, their own purposes, and their own wills. They are dead to self, Satan, and worldly aspirations. It is Christ Jesus who lives in them, leading them and guiding them by Holy Spirit, to do Father's will – not their own will.

Galatians 2:20 Paul said, " I am crucified with Christ. Nevertheless I live, yet not I, but Christ lives in me: and the life which I now live in the flesh I live by the faith of the Son of God, who loved me, and gave himself for me."It was Christ living in Paul. Paul was dead to himself, his own life, his own will. He surrendered everything to Christ and was trusting Christ fully. He was holding nothing back. Jesus was Lord of Paul's entire life. Is He Lord of your life?

How much of your life have you really surrendered to Jesus? Is he Lord over your family, your children, your finances, your own purposes, your own will, your entire life? If not, you need to surrender fully and trust in Jesus with it all. People sing, " All to Jesus I surrender, all to him I freely give," and they refuse to trust him with their entire lives. " I surrender all, I surrender all," they say, but don't mean it.

The reason Christians don't walk in victory over the devil is that they refuse to fully die to themselves, let go of their lives and Trust Jesus with everything. They refuse to fully surrender their lives.

Take a look at Revelation 12:7-11, the devil, the old dragon and his angels are cast down onto the earth by Michael and his angels. In verse 11, the Bible says " And they overcame him (the devil, Satan), by the blood of the lamb (Jesus), and by the Word of their testimony: (confessing Christ as Savior), and they loved not their lives unto death." They gave their whole lives to Jesus. They held nothing back. Every area of their life was fully surrendered to Jesus. There was no area of their life where," self and Satan", were on the throne. Jesus was Lord over their entire life. Any areas you refuse to surrender to Jesus are under the control of self and Satan. If Satan has a foothold in your life, you will not get victory over him. Self-denial is the key to victory over Satan. Self-denial and full surrender to Jesus, bring full victory.

> Mark 8:34-35 Jesus said, "Whosoever will come after me, let him deny himself and take up his cross and follow me. For whosoever will save his life shall lose it; but whosoever shall lose his life for my sake and the gospels, the same shall save it."

Until Christians surrender their entire lives to Jesus, He cannot trust them with the Greater Glory. They would misuse it.

While in Gilgal, Kenya, I asked the Lord, "Where is your Isaiah 60 Glory?" The Lord said "Ask my people this question: How can I trust you with My Glory, if you won't trust me with your life?" The Lord needs more people to fully surrender to Him, so they will be able to carry His Isaiah 60 Glory.

To Surrender Fully To Jesusl, Pray: "Father God I repent Of living for myself and hanging onto my own will and life. I give you me – my body, my soul, my spirit. I give you my emotions, feelings, and will. I give you my family, my finances, my own agendas, and my own will, and my own life. I don't want my will anymore, I Surrender it to you along with this life. Use this life to your glory, honor, and praise. I give it all to you and your purposes, in Jesus Name, amen. Sometimes God calls you to do something and the Devil tells his people to try to get you to doubt what God has told you to do. Listen to God and obey Him no matter what.

> Acts 7:23-28 Moses was 40 years old and went to visit his brethren , the children of Israel. He saw one of them suffer wrong and killed the Egyptian: " For he supposed his brethren would have understood how that God by his hand would deliver them: but they understood not." In verse 27 one said to Moses, "Who made you a ruler and a judge over us?" In verse 35 " This Moses whom they refused, saying, who made you a ruler and a judge? The same did God send to be a ruler and a deliver by the hand of the Angel which appeared to him in the bush."

Notice that people didn't realize the call of God on Moses's life. Maybe someone doesn't realize the call of God on your life. God sees your heart. Stay faithful to God. He will raise you up, in his perfect time. They cannot stop God's plan for your life. God will do it. God has your destiny. Through God, you will fulfill it.

In Acts 8:5, Philip went to Samaria and preached Christ. He confronted Simon, a sorcerer, who had bewitched the people. Simon wanted the power to lay hands on people to impart the Holy Ghost and offered the disciples money. Philip rebuked him in Acts 8: 21-24 and told Simon to repent. The Holy Ghost Power could not be purchased with money.

Acts 9: 36-41 a man had been sick with the palsy eight years. Jesus made him whole.

Acts 9:36-41 Peter prayed for a dead disciple named Tabitha (yes, there were many female disciples). In verse 40, Peter put the weeping people outside. Then he kneeled down and said, "Tabitha arise." And she opened her eyes and lived. Many believed in the Lord.

While in Buteri, Kenya, a five year old boy died of malaria. His mother had carried her son, who was ill for a few weeks, to the church believing God would heal him. The boy died as she came onto the church property. She was screaming, " My boy is dead, my boy is dead!"

Pastor Richard Ungudi, his wife and I were having tea, after the service. As we ran outside, the Holy Spirit-filled me and I rebuked the spirit of death off of the boy. Then I said , "In Jesus name, you will live and you will not die. You will fulfill your days on the earth and they will not be shortened, in Jesus name!" The boy's eyes opened, he sat up and was restored to life and health, by the power of God, in Jesus Name. It was a current day " Resurrection Miracle." The same Holy Spirit that operated through Peter can operate through us today.

Acts 12: 1-11 Herod killed James the brother of John with the sword. He put Peter in prison and delivered him to four quaternions of soldiers to keep him; intending after Easter to bring him forth to the people. Continual prayer was made by the church for Peter. (Notice that Easter was a pagan holiday that even Herod celebrated to the fertility god.) I always say, "Happy Resurrection Sunday," because I celebrate Christ's Resurrection-not the fertility god.

In verse 6, Peter was sleeping between two soldiers, bound with two chains; and the keepers before the door kept the prison. In verse 7," the angel of the Lord came upon Peter, a light shined in the prison and the angel smote Peter on the side and raised him up. The angel said, " Arise up quickly" and his chains fell off from his hands. The angel said, " Gird yourself, and put on your sandals. Cast your garment about yourself, and follow me. Peter went out, and followed him, and did not know it was true which was done by the angel. he thought he saw a vision. When they were past the first and the second ward, they came to the iron gate that led into the city and it opened to them of his own accord; and they went out and passed on through one street and the angel departed from Peter."

Let's think about this. The angel appeared in Peter's cell, lit up the prison, woke Peter up and raised him up from his sleep. He was in the innermost part of the prison, since he and the angel had to pass through two ward's to get to the iron gate that led into the city. Peter was bound by two chains and was sleeping between two soldiers. There were keepers at the prison doors. The chains fell off Peter's hands. The two guards in the cell with him, never woke up, even when the light shone in the cell. It was as if Peter were invisible. He passed the keepers at the door who failed to see him. He walked through two ward's with guards and none of them saw him. The iron gate to the city opened by itself. It was a miraculous escape.

> In Acts 12:11 Peter said, the Lord has sent his angel, and has delivered me out of the hand of Herod and from all the expectation of the Jews."

If we study Acts chapters 20 through chapter 28, we see that many prophets warned Paul not to go to Jerusalem. They warned him by Holy Spirit, what would befall him there and begged him not to go there.

> In Acts 20: 22-24, Paul said, " And now, behold, I go bound in the spirit unto Jerusalem, not knowing the things that shall befall me there: save that the Holy Ghost witnessed in every city, saying that bonds and afflictions abide me. But none of these things move me, neither do I count my life dear unto myself, so that I might finish my course with joy and the ministry, which I have received of the Lord Jesus, to testify the gospel of the grace of God."

In Acts 21: 10-14 a prophet named Agabus spoke that the Jews would deliver Paul unto the hands of the Gentiles. Paul answered, " Why do You weep and break my heart? For I am ready not only to be bound but also to die at Jerusalem for the Name of the Lord Jesus. And when he would not be persuaded, we ceased, saying, the will of the Lord be done."

Paul had a choice of listening to the humans who loved him and begged him not to go, or listening to the Holy Spirit who was calling him to go. If Paul did not go, he would have been busy preaching the gospel everywhere. He would not have had the time to sit and write many books of the New Testament Scriptures, given by Holy Spirit. In prison, he wrote much of the New Testament, and witnessed to Romans.

In Acts 25: He spoke to Festus, Agrippa, and Bernice, about Jesus. Then he was put on a boat with other prisoners to set sail for Rome. Contrary winds came up and it was dangerous to sail. They were lost at sea, tossed with a tempest, neither the sun nor stars appeared for many days and most of them lost hope of being saved. An angel of the Lord spoke to Paul in Acts 27:24 saying, "Fear not, Paul : you must be brought before Caesar and God has given you all of them that sail with you."

In Acts 27:33 everyone on the ship fasted for 14 days. In verse 34 Paul took bread, gave thanks to God and ate. They ate also. They got on the Island called Melita. Acts 28:1-6 Paul was putting wood on the fire. A venomous beast hung on Paul's hand. The people expected Paul to swell up and die suddenly.

When they saw that no harm came to Paul, they thought he was a God. The Father of Publias, (the chief man of the Island), was sick of a fever and bloody flux. Paul prayed, laid hands on him and healed him. Many others were also healed.

When Paul did arrive in Rome, Paul preached Jesus and many people believed, but some believed not.

Acts 28: 30-31 "And Paul dwelt two years in his own hired house, and received all that came in unto him, preaching the kingdom of God, and teaching those things which concern the Lord Jesus Christ, with all confidence, no man forbidding him."

While preaching and teaching in a village in Uganda, a woman handed me a bag left at her door by a witch doctor. The man terrorized the town people with his occult practices and the objects, hexes and witchcraft items that he would leave at their doors. The woman said, " He told me if I get rid of the bag, I'll go crazy. I don't know what to do with it." I said, " In Jesus name, you will not go crazy. Give it to me." While I was preaching the Gospel of Jesus Christ, I opened the witchcraft bag and dumped its chicken feet, bird feathers, and other items on the Crusade platform, doused it with gasoline and burnt it all up. I preached that my Jesus is the real God and His power is greater than any witch doctor, wizard, devil, and Satan himself. Many Souls came to faith in Jesus, that day. The angry witch doctor planned to murder me the next day. He began to climb up on the platform, in back of me, while I was preaching. The pastors grabbed him and wrestled him to the ground. A giant knife fell out of his clothing. He got away from the pastors and ran in front of the platform. I pointed my finger at him and said, " In the name of Jesus you are bound, you will not come near this crusade ground again, in Jesus name." With that, the people who he used to terrorize, chased him off of the property. When I gave an altar call, many people received Jesus Christ as their Savior and Lord. The town was delivered from the fear of the witch doctor. I was still there for three more days doing crusades and growing the new believers in the faith.

One night, I was in my hotel room in Kisumu, Kenya. I awoke to the sound of someone stomping, growling, and huffing and puffing around my bed. Holy Spirit said, " It is Satan." I said, " Satan in the Name of Jesus, I command you to get out of this hotel room now and never come back." I got out of the bed turned on the light, saw that Satan was gone, shut the light, went back to bed and back to sleep.

We need to remember that at the Name of Jesus, every knee must bow including Satan's knees. Our God is God –ALL POWERFUL, and ALMIGHTY. HE is the CREATOR OF HEAVEN AND EARTH. Satan is just a fallen angel. He is a created being. The book of Acts has no official ending. The miracles, signs, and wonders are still happening today. The giftings of the Holy Spirit are as real today as they always were.

> John 14:12 Jesus said, " He that believes on me, the works that I do shall he do also, and Greater Works than these shall you do; because I go unto my Father."

I am believing for the Greater Works. I am believing to pray for missing limbs and watch them grow out of stumps. It happened at the Azusa Street Revival a hundred years ago. It happened at A. A. Allen's tent meetings down south in the 1950's and 1960's, and it can happen today.

> Ezekiel chapter 37 is a great passage of scripture to study. It is about the Valley of Dry Bones. For years, I had heard pastors preach on the valley of dry bones, But I never heard what God revealed to me, one night in my prayer room .

My Bible fell open to Ezekiel 37 and I reread it. Then God said to me, " Daughter, do you realize how many miracles I did, in the valley of dry bones? I gave dry bones new brains, new hearts, lungs, kidneys, immune systems, digestive systems, intestines, arms, legs, feet, hands, skin, faces, eyes, ears, hair, etc...."

For about an hour, I sat stunned and awed by God. The Revelation he gave me was so amazing and so exciting, I couldn't go back to sleep. The same God who gave all these miracles to dry bones, is the same God who can perform these Miracles today. The dry bones became a full standing army of people. They had brand new everything. He took dead, Dry Bones, brought them back to life and formed people from them. If He could do it then, He can do it now.

For many years I have been believing for people's limbs to grow out of stumps. Every time I see a person is missing an arm or leg, I ask Holy Spirit, " Is it now?" I hear Him say, " Not yet, but at the appointed time." I know he has set a time, and these Miracles will come forth. I'm like a child at a candy store window saying, " Can I have the candy now? Can I have these miracles happen now?"

Nothing is impossible for God. So far, I can testify that I saw God heal a broken finger in seconds. A man whose organs shut down was healed overnight. The next day he walked into the meeting totally healed. The Lord healed barren wombs, back issues, babies of malaria, cancerous tumors disappeared, fibroid tumors disappeared, a dead boy was raised, drunks were saved and delivered from alcoholism, demoniacs were delivered, bondages were broken and entire churches were set free of tribal customs and traditional hatreds that were not of God. Unforgiveness and hatred were broken, depression was broken, tribal hatreds were broken, demonic rituals were repented of and broken by the power of Holy Spirit. Lies and deceptions were broken off of God's people.

The book of Acts continues on as Holy Spirit operates in us and through us to advance God's Kingdom on planet Earth. " Those who are led by the Spirit of God, are the Sons of God. Nothing is impossible for our God. Nothing is impossible for those who believe.

CHAPTER 13
FEAR IS A
DEMONIC SPIRIT

Years ago, someone gave me a definition of fear. Fear is " False Evidence Appearing Real." There are 365 "Fear Nots", in the Bible - one for every day of the year.

> 2 Timothy 1:7 "For God has not given us a spirit of fear; but of power, and of love, and of a sound mind." In this scripture, we see that fear is a demonic spirit. It doesn't come from God. It comes from Satan to hinder, cripple, and destroy people's ability to freely function and enjoy their lives.

For many years, I was terrorized by "The fear of man", "The fear of what people would think of me", "The fear of having to get up in front of people to speak", and the "Fear of Oral School Reports".

Having to render an oral report before a class of fellow students kept me in dread, sleeplessness, and misery for weeks before the report was due. As the time for me to present my report neared, I was totally miserable.

It all began in kindergarten when mean children made fun of my Boston accent and teased me. We had moved from M.A. to R.I. The accents were not the same. After that, I was the quietest child in school. I stayed silent . I would never volunteer to speak for fear of being made fun of or laughed at. I had a few close friends that studied hard, went to church, and stayed out of trouble.

During the years of 1993-1996, there were Holy Spirit Revival Meetings going on in a church across the river. The Holy Spirit moved mightily in the hearts and lives of God's people. He ministered to each person individually. One day, while on the floor, in His Presence, I thought, " Lord, please deliver me from the fear of man, the fear of what people think of me, and the fear of speaking in front of people. I don't want this fear any more." That night, the Lord took away all the fear and gave me Boldness.

Years later, He sent me to Africa to do crusades, preach in Churches, preach in Camp Meetings, do Pastor's Conferences, do deliverance ministry, appear on Sayre TV out of Eldoret, Kenya and local television in N.Y. and preach on radio etc...

Psalm 56:4 "In God I will praise his word, in God I have put my trust; I will not fear what flesh can do to me."

When we study 1 Samuel Chapter 15:1-24, we see that Saul's excuse for not obeying God, was "because I feared the people, and obeyed their voice." The fear of man brings a snare. It ensnared Saul.

Psalm 23 is a very familiar Psalm to most people, "The Lord is My Shepherd." In verse 4, it says, "Yea through I walk through the valley of the shadow of death, I will fear no evil: for thou art with me; your rod and your staff, they comfort me."

Why are so many people afraid of a germ called Covid 19? Why should God's people be afraid of anything or anyone? Why should God's people fear death? Why should God's people fear riding in an airplane? Crossing a bridge? etc... They should fear God and depart from evil. Any other type of fear is a demonic spirit.

Psalm 27:1-2 "The Lord is my light and my salvation; whom shall I fear? the Lord is the strength of my life; of whom shall I be afraid?" We can also ask, "Of what shall I be afraid?" Fear is the opposite of faith. Fear robs faith and gives way to doubt and unbelief.

We can see this in Matthew 14:22-32. The disciples had gotten into a ship to get to the other shore. The ship was in the midst of the sea, tossed with waves and the wind was contrary. Jesus was walking on the sea. In verse 28-29, "Peter said, If it is you Lord, bid me to come to you on the water. Jesus said, Come. And when Peter had come down out of the ship, he walked on water, to go to Jesus. But when he saw the boisterous wind, he was afraid; and beginning to sink, he cried, saying Lord, save me. And immediately Jesus stretched forth his hand, and caught him, and said unto him, "O you of little faith, wherefore did you doubt?"

Peter had a lot of faith to step out of the ship and walk on water, when his natural mind was telling him that liquid water could not hold him up. While his eyes were on Jesus, he could do supernatural things. When he took his eyes off of Jesus and reverted to his flesh, he sank. The moment he took his eyes off of Jesus and looked at his surroundings (the wind and the waves), fear set in , and then doubt. The main weapons the devil uses against Christians are fear, doubt, and unbelief. As I said before, fear is the opposite of Faith.

Lets look at some common fears that people are plagued with by the devil and his agents. The news media spews fear constantly. It prays on people's fears and emotions and is used mightily, by Satan, to rob people of their freedom to "Fear Not", and enjoy their lives.

Fear of "Rejection", will keep you from giving your heart to anyone. It will keep you on guard all the time and prevent you from ever letting anyone get close to you. It will keep you from trusting anyone or receiving any genuine love, even God's Love.

Fear of "Failure", will keep you from trying anything new. It will keep you from opening a business, trying for a promotion, going to job interviews, attending college, etc... If you believe you will fail, you are defeated before you start. It will cause you to sabotage your entire future.

God's Word says in Philippians 4:13, "I can do all things through Christ who strengthens me." Do you believe God can't lie? If you believe God's Word and step out in faith, you will see God bring amazing things to pass in your life.

Here is a challenge for you. Put Philippians 4:13 written out, on your refrigerator or somewhere where you will see it often. Read it out loud, several times a day for three months or until that truth gets imbedded into your heart and you believe it. Then act on it. It will change your life. As this truth gets into your heart and life, you will be amazed at what the Lord says you can do and enables you to do. You will not fail.

When God called me to do evangelism in African villages, mountains, deserts, churches, camp meetings, Pastor's Conferences etc... The devil told me, "You can't do this. You haven't attended such and such Bible College. You have never preached in public before. What if you get tongue-tied? What if the African people don't like you?" "What ifs", are always from the devil. If God has told you to do something, don't listen to the "What ifs", of the devil. Step out in faith and trust God. God will enable you to do it. He has already trained you and readied you for His Call on your life.

> James 4:7-8 "Submit yourselves to God, Resist the devil and he will flee from you. Draw near to God and he will draw near to you." When God calls you to do something, believe you can do it. To believe "You Can't do it" when God says, "You Can", is doubt and unbelief. Be prepared. The devil will try to use people (relatives and friends) to talk you out of obeying God. Just obey God. My mother gave me an article about the diseases in Africa, the crime rates, the animal attacks, etc... before I went to Africa. I ripped it up and threw it in the garbage. I trusted Jesus and never read the article.

> In Matthew 16: 21-23, Jesus told his disciples what he would suffer in Jerusalem. Peter began to rebuke Jesus saying, "This shall not happen to you." Jesus rebuked Peter and said, "Get thee behind me Satan: you are an offense to me: you savor not the things that be of God, but those that be of men." Satan was trying to discourage Jesus from obeying Father's Will. He will try to use people to keep you from obeying God's Will for your life. Obey God.

Satan will always use someone close to you, even a pastor, to speak words of fear, doubt, discouragement and unbelief to keep you from obeying God's Will for your life. If you know the Bible and can discern the Voice of Jesus, obey God. God will never tell you to do something contrary to His Word. He would never tell you to steal, lie, or murder someone. He is concerned with the salvation, deliverance, and healing of people. Just Obey God. Do God's Will. Have Faith.

Fear of Heights will keep you from flying a plane, being a stewardess, a construction worker, climbing a ladder, mountain climbing, seeing Hawaii, Aruba, etc...(you could always take a cruise, unless you are "Afraid you will drown in the sea).

If you are "Afraid of Bridges", you will drive miles out of the way to avoid crossing a bridge over water. I had an aunt who was afraid to cross a bridge over water. One day she didn't realize she was on the bridge until she was half-way across. She panicked and stopped her car. Traffic began to mount up behind her. People got irritated and started honking their horns, blasting the noise everywhere. In frustration, the man in the car in back of hers got out and said, "Lady what is your problem?" A passenger in his car had to get into my aunt's car to drive her the rest of the way across the bridge. Fear is crippling.

Another relative wouldn't leave her apartment for the last ten years of her life. She was "afraid of being mugged" and "afraid of someone breaking in and stealing her possessions, while she was out." She lived a miserable, lonely existence because of her fears. Satan robbed her of the ability to enjoy her life.

Some marriages break up over fear. A woman would never go on a vacation with her husband because she was afraid of flying. Her husband's family were all in Puerto Rico. He went there on vacation by himself. Eventually, he met another woman and divorced his wife. If she had gone on vacations with her husband, that other woman wouldn't have been able to tempt him to stray. It is not good for a husband and wife to take separate vacations. They need quality time together-not apart.

"Fear of Man", will keep you from sharing your Christian Faith with anyone. Fear of man, will cause you to obey people over God. Fear of man will cause you to compromise your faith. It will keep you from speaking up or speaking out against morally wrong issues. You will be so "Afraid of Offending Someone", that you will Offend God by your silence.

"Fear of losing your tax-exempt status", will cause pastors to be ear ticklers that make people feel good on their way to hell. These compromised pastors will never preach that abortion is murder, that gayness is a sexual sin , along with fornication, adultery, pornography, sodomy, homosexuality, lesbianism, bi-sexuality, bestiality, transgender, cross-dressing, etc.... They will never preach the Truth of The Word of God. God will hold these unfaithful pastors accountable for the souls they destroy.

"Fear of Not Being In Control", keeps pastors in their flesh, and not allowing God, the Holy Spirit, to come into their churches to minister to His People. They pre-program the entire service and use the whole time for man-made programs, rituals, and agendas. They pencil God out with their man made, controlling agendas.

Only God, the Holy Spirit, knows what each individual person needs, at any given time. He can bring the emotional pain of someone's abusive childhood to the surface and heal them through their tears. He can remove the spirit of heaviness and depression from them and give them joy and laughter. He can bind up the broken hearted. He can deliver people from the bondages of drugs, alcoholism, gambling, lust, perversion, etc...He can heal their wounded spirits and souls as well as their physical ailments. He can make them whole in body, soul, and spirit. He can remove the sorrow and grief from the human heart and put joy and gladness in. He can pour out God's Love into a human heart and soul, in a deeper way, assuring a person that He Loves Them. He can show a person His Plan and His Purpose as they lie on the floor in His Presence. There is nothing like the Presence of God. I would rather be on the floor, in God's Presence, than anywhere else on planet earth.

> Isaiah 61:1-3 "The Spirit of the Lord God is upon me (the Holy Spirit was upon Jesus); because the Lord has anointed me to preach good tidings unto the meek; he has sent me to bind up the broken hearted, to proclaim liberty to the captives, and the opening of the prison to them that are bound; To proclaim the acceptable year of the Lord, and the day of vengeance of our God; to comfort all that mourn; To appoint unto them that mourn in Zion, to give unto them beauty for ashes, the oil of joy for mourning, the garment of praise for the spirit of heaviness; that they might be called trees of righteousness, the planting of the Lord, that He might be glorified." The Holy Spirit that was upon Jesus is upon the believers in Christ now.

Unless the Holy Spirit is allowed back into the churches and pastors get out of the way, God's people will never be changed into the Trees of Righteousness to glorify Him in the way He deserves to be glorified. The Holy Spirit changes us from glory to glory into the image of Christ. Pastors need to be Holy Spirit Led, or they need to get out of the pulpits. We Need Holy Ghost Preachers who will welcome God's Spirit to move upon God's people. We need God the Holy Spirit back into our Churches, Now! We need the Greater Signs, Wonders, and Miracles that Jesus said we will do, to come forth. The flesh profits nothing. The Spirit is Life. We need the Bible preached, the entire Bible!

We sing, "Holy Spirit You are Welcome in this Place", but when He begins to move on people, we get frightened and close down the service. Why? He is God the Holy Spirit. He can do more in a human heart, soul, or spirit than years of counseling and therapy could ever do. He can get to the root of the problem and fix it.

Pastors Let Go Of God's Sheep! Get Out of The Way of God's Holy Spirit and let Him change His People, heal His people, Minister to His people, and get them ready for God's Plan and Purposes. Let Holy Spirit give them fresh revelation into the Word, fresh vision, more mantles, more anointing, more of God's Love, Peace, and Joy. You cannot get into the depths of a person's heart, soul, and spirit man, to heal, restore, refresh, encourage, deliver, anoint, convict, etc... and do what they need. There are people in your pews that are wounded, hurting, addicted, suffering from generational curses, suffering from fear, rejection, depression, discouragement, ailments, emotional pain and hurt, etc... You are harming and destroying God's Sheep. HE will hold you accountable.

> 11 Corinthians 3:17-18 "Now the Lord is that Spirit, and where the Spirit of the Lord is, there is liberty. But we all, with open face beholding as in a glass the glory of the Lord, are changed into the same image from glory to glory, even as by the Spirit of the Lord."

> Romans 8:14-17 "For as many as are led by the Spirit of God, they are the sons of God. For you have not received the spirit of bondage again to fear, but you have received the Spirit of Adoption, whereby we cry, Abba, Father. The Spirit Himself bears witness with our spirit, that we are the children of God. And if children, then heirs; heirs of God and joint-heirs with Christ."

The people who are led by the Spirit of God, are Sons of God, free from fear, adopted by Father God and joint heirs with Christ. Who are the people who are not led by the Spirit of God? Are they really sons of God, if they are walking in the flesh? The flesh profits nothing. The Spirit is life.

Hebrews 2:14-15 "Forasmuch then as the children are partakers of flesh and blood, Jesus himself took part of the same; that through death he might destroy him that had the power of death that is, the devil. And deliver them who through fear of death were all their lifetime subject to bondage."

Through faith in Jesus Christ and the empowering and leading of Holy Spirit, we are free from bondages to fear, even the fear of death. Through Christ, we know we have eternal life. To be absent in the body is to be present with Jesus.

John 11:25-26 Jesus said, "I am the resurrection, and the life; he that believes in me, though he be dead, yet shall he live: And whosoever lives and believes in me shall never die." We will Live Forever.

What Is The Remedy For These Demonic Spirits of Fear? How do we get rid of them?

In Matthew 18:18, Jesus said, "Whatsoever you shall bind on earth shall be bound in heaven: and whatsoever you shall loose on earth shall be loosed in heaven." Jesus gave his people the power to bind demons and cast them out , in Jesus Name. We have Jesus Name (authority in His Name), and the Power of Holy Spirit to enforce our words spoken, in Jesus Name. All demons, all principalities, all powers, all rulers of darkness, and even Satan himself, have to bow before the Name of Jesus. Every knee will bow to our Jesus.

While in a village, during the night, I had to use the outhouse. It was located about 60 feet from the house, down a dirt path. I put on my robe, my shoes, grabbed my flashlight and proceeded to walk down the path. I just got inside the outhouse and closed the door, when giant claws began tearing at the outside of the door. Fear began filling me as I realized those claws could have been on my skin. Then, Holy Spirit reminded me of 2 Timothy 1:7, "God has not given me a spirit of fear, but of power, love and a sound mind." I quoted the scripture. Then I said," You demons of fear, leave me now, in Jesus Name." Immediately the fear left me. Then I said, " Father God, send an angel to chase this creature back into the woods, in Jesus Name. Amen." I waited five minutes, walked back to the house, praised Jesus and went back to bed.

You can speak to the demons of fear and command them to leave you, in Jesus Name. Amen. Cast them out of yourself, any time you feel afraid of any one or anything. If someone is threatening you, just speak the Name of Jesus and the demons in them will run away. They flee from Jesus.

We can ask God to send His angels to help us at any time. He sent an angel to chase the creature back into the woods for me. He will help you also.

FEAR GOD AND DEPART FROM EVIL

Matthew 10:28 "And fear not them which can kill the body, but are not able to kill the soul: but rather fear him, which is able to destroy both soul and body in hell." Don't fear man. Fear God, who can cast body and soul into hell.

Yes, there is a place called hell. Ezekiel 31:16-18 speaks of hell, which is located in the neither parts of the earth. It is called hell, the pit, and the center of the earth. Scripture tells us that Pharoah and all his multitudes are there. After they drowned in the Red Sea, they went down to hell. Since they rejected God (the real God), served false gods of Egypt, enslaved and persecuted God's people, trapped God's people by the Red Sea wanting to murder them: the Judgment of God came upon them. IT only took a few minutes and they were all dead and in hell forever. You can read the entire story in Exodus 15.

Hollywood has produced a lot of lying movies that say, "Everyone is a child of God, there is no hell, Jesus was just a man, Jesus was a sinner, God has no Wrath, everyone goes to heaven no matter what they do, etc...These ridiculous ideas are crazy and are contrary with God's Holy Bible.

The TRUTH is found in the parable of the Sower in Matthew 13:37-43. The wheat are God's people. The tares are Satan's people, who will be burnt in the fire. The wheat will be saved and gathered into God's barns.

John 3:36 "He that believes on the Son, (Jesus), has everlasting life: and he that believes not the Son of God shall not see life; but the wrath of God abides on him."

Romans 1:18 "For the wrath of God is revealed from heaven against all ungodliness and unrighteousness of men who hold the truth in unrighteousness."

Any pastor, minister, preacher... who knows God's truth and refuses to preach it, will be held accountable to God. Instead of preaching the truth to bring people to repentance and a right walk with God, they keep silent to please man. They allow people to sit in their churches, tithe their money to the church, have unconfessed sin in their lives, and perish in their wickedness, because they don't love them enough to tell them the truth. Fear God and preach His Truth.

The Karl Marx, Satanic ideologies of Communism, Socialism, Racism, CRT, BLM, and Nazism, atheism, KKK, occultism, perversion, sex-trafficking of children, abortion/ murders of babies Jesus is forming in the womb, media lies, Darwinism, Evolution lies, Fornication, adulteries, pornography, transgender, many genders, woks, New Age Movement, and other Satanic lies are being promoted in our schools, our colleges, on TV, radio, Movies etc...as good things.

When are you pastors, preachers, priests, and ministers going to STAND UP FOR GOD AND PREACH HIS HOLY BIBLICAL TRUTHS? Why are you keeping silent and allowing Satan to destroy the youth of our Nation? When are you going to FIGHT THE GOOD FIGHT OF FAITH? When are you going to be a GOOD SOLDIER IN GOD'S ARMY and teach others spiritual warfare? Ezekiel 3:16-21 says that if we stay silent and don't warn the wicked, they will die in their sins, but God will hold us accountable.

Jesus confronted the scribes and Pharisees many times. In Matthew 23:23, Jesus said, "You outwardly appear righteous to men, but within you are full of hypocrisy and iniquity." He called them white-washed tombs full of dead men's bones. He continually confronted them with their stealing of widows houses, and making long prayers in the marketplace just to be seen of men.

Have you bought the devil's lie that the people of God should always be meek and passive and should never confront anyone, or make waves? The lie is that you are judging someone by telling them they are in sin? By their fruits you will know whether or not they are really of God. We can see the sin, judge it, and reprove and correct the sinner. If we really love God and love people, we must tell them the truth whether they like what we say or not. If they get offended at the Word of God, they are not walking right or living right. The Word of God is supposed to instruct, correct, reprove, and change us to be like Jesus.

May God deliver the entire Body of Christ from the "fear of man", "fear of what people will think", "fear of persecution", "fear of rejection", "fear of covid-19", "fear of sharing the Gospel of Jesus Christ with others", "fear of germs", "fear of dying", "Fear of losing members", "fear of the media-mob that are on their way to hell", "fear of retaliation", "fear of witches, wizards, demons, the devil, occultists etc...", "fear of heights", "fear of failure", "fear of things that have not happened yet", "fear of Satan", and all other fears, in Jesus Name. Amen!

May the Body of Christ fear God with a holy reverence that will cause them to put all sin out of their lives, read and know God's Holy Bible, be led by Holy Spirit, be baptized in the Holy Spirit, and really honor Jesus in their thoughts, words, and deeds, in Jesus Name. Amen."

CHAPTER 14
STOP THE MEDIA'S HATE

We are living in a time when evil is called "good", and good is called "evil". This wicked brain-washing, name calling, woks, CRT, lies, deceptions, cancel culture, promotion of racism, white privilege lies, slave mentality, division, being offended at everyone and everything, must stop now, in Jesus Name. People are acting like spoiled five years olds. If everything and everyone else offends them, maybe they should be in an institution for the insane. It is not normal to find fault with everyone and everything around you and riot when you don't get your own way. When are they going to grow up and act like adults?

> Isaiah 5:20 "Woe unto them that call evil "good", and good "evil"; that put darkness for light, and light for darkness; that put bitter for sweet and sweet for bitter!"

The hateful, wicked, media was responsible for the Holocaust where millions of Jewish people were seized, imprisoned, tortured, and murdered. They were removed from their homes, their families, their friends, their possessions, and forced onto trains that took some to prison and others to burn in ovens. Wives never knew what became of their husbands or children. Men were separated from their families. Children were murdered. Many Jewish women bravely chose to die with their children rather then let their children die alone.

The media, in Germany, poisoned the German people's hearts against the Jews by radio and newspapers. The Jews were called, "useless eaters", "worthless", "useless people", and other de-humanizing names to detract from the fact that they were human beings made in the image of God. The lying campaign against the Jews went on and on, until most German people believed the lies and blamed the Jews for everything that went wrong in their lives. Any problems, any lack of things, anything that went wrong, any difficulties …were all the fault of the Jews. The media convinced the German people that the Jews had no right to live. So they allowed the Jews to be murdered.

Satan hates the Jewish people because the seed of the woman, (Jesus), who would crush Satan's head, was placed in the womb of a Jewish woman named Mary. Jesus came in the lineage of David, a Jew. Both the Old Testament and the New Testament Scriptures were written by holy Jewish men, as they were moved by the Holy Ghost. The original twelve disciples of Jesus were all Jews. Jesus was nursed by a Jewish woman. He was raised a Jew and celebrated the Jewish Feast Days. Christians should stand with Israel and Bless the Jewish People. We would have no faith in Christ, no Bible, no Words of God to live by, etc... if it were not for the faithful Jews who spread the Gospel and preserved the Word of God. We owe them a lot of thanks.

Some people hate the Jews and call them, "Christ Killers." Jesus Christ died on that cross for sinners. We all nailed him to the cross because we all have sinned and fallen short of the glory of God. If Jesus didn't die on the cross for the sins of His Creation (mankind), we would all die in our sins and be condemned to hell. He chose to lay his life down for us. He could have called twelve legions of angels to stop the crucifixion, but then the scriptures would not have been fulfilled and mankind would not have been redeemed. (Isaiah 53, Psalm 22 and other scriptures had to be fulfilled by Jesus). Otherwise He wouldn't have been the Lamb of God who would take away the sins of the world. Thank Father God for sending Jesus to die in our place, for our sins, so we could have eternal life. Don't Forget-Jesus Rose From The Dead. He's Alive! He's Alive! He's Alive forever more!

God still says, "Pray for the peace of Jerusalem. " The Church did not replace the Jews. Replacement theology is wrong. God still loves the Jews and always will. Those who Bless Abraham, (the Jews), will be blessed and those who curse Abraham, (the Jews), will be cursed.

When America influenced Israel to give up the Gaza Strip for (so-called peace), one million Jews lost their homes, their vineyards, their neighbors, their businesses, etc... and were forced to evacuate and let the Palestinians have Gaza. Right away, a hurricane hit Louisiana and one million Americans were displaced for some months. The Palestinians who moved into Gaza burnt down the homes, the vineyards, and destroyed everything the Jews worked hard for. They are now using the Gaza Strip to lob bombs and kites with fiery tails into Israel to set fire to homes and crops within Israel's boarders. Of course, our lying media refuses to tell the truth about anything.

THE MEDIA'S HATRED AND AFRICAN GENOCIDES

Both the genocides in Rwanda and Burundi were a result of a planned strategy, by the media, to promote hatred in the Hutu people's hearts against the Tutsi people. The hatred was deliberately spewed through the radio and through newspapers and publications to poison the Hutu people against their own family members, friends, and neighbors who were Tutsis. Prior to the media's hate promotions, both tribes of people intermarried, lived in peace side by side, worked together, went to college together, played together, and got along well.

Satan used the media ,in Africa, as he did in Germany, to destroy human lives by implanting and promoting hatred, to get people to murder other people. Satan hates people because we are all made by God in God's own image. Satan wants to steal, kill and destroy human beings in any way he can.

When the Hutu Presidents of Rwanda and Burundi were murdered (probably by other power-hungry Hutu's) the Tutsi people were blamed. Radio broadcasts and publications screamed for revenge on the Tutsi people and the horrible genocides happened. The media's hate, implanted in the Hutu's hearts, bore the fruit of MURDER. A million Tutsis' in Rwanda and half a million Tutsis' in Burundi were murdered. Their murders were incited, fueled and planned by a Satanic media. Whoever paid the media to spew the hatred caused the genocides in both nations.

Hutu husbands murdered their Tutsi wives and children. Hutu college students murdered their Tutsi classmates. Hutu professors murdered the Tutsi professors. I saw the effects of the genocide when I was in Rwanda and Burundi in 1999. In front of Rwanda University are two huge graves with blue and white banners about the genocide written on them.. There are 300 college students and professors buried in each grave (600 people murdered at the college alone). Any Hutu trying to hide a Tutsi, was also murdered. Dead bodies were everywhere. Even Churches were filled with the dead, decaying bodies of the slain.

While traveling through the mountainous roads of Rwanda and Burundi, I saw the remains of many houses where families once lived and children once played. They were now heaps of rubble; broken down brick walls with evidence of bullet holes, mortars, and grenades. I knew that the owners of those homes were probably murdered in the genocide. I wept as I realized how horrible hatred is.

The people who did survive the genocide will never enjoy family picnics with their spouse, get to attend their children's graduations from school or college, and never be able to walk their daughters down the aisle at their wedding . The horrible grief, sadness, memories of the genocide and loneliness haunt them continually. Some of the survivors are the only ones left of their entire family, neighborhood, or village. The Media Caused these Genocides.

While in Rwanda, I got to minister to a woman who saw her mother thrown in an outhouse pit. The Hutu men opened the top of the outhouse hole and threw her mother into the hole and buried her alive, in the human waste. Many people were raped, beaten, slashed with knives, blown up with grenades, etc... The Hutu people, full of the media's poisonous hatred, were used by Satan to destroy many innocent lives.

> 1 John 4:7-11 "Beloved let us love one another; for love is of God; and every one who loves is born of God and knows God. He that loves not knows not God; for God is love. In this was manifested the love of God toward us, because God sent his only begotten Son into the world, that we might live through him. Herein is love, not that we loved God, but that he loved us, and sent his Son to be the propitiation for our sins. Beloved, if God so loved us, we ought also to love one another."

If God is Love and he who loves is of God, then he who Hates, is of Satan. The wicked media that spews hate is of Satan. Lies, false accusations, Woks, Communism, Socialism, Marxism, Darwinism, Evolution, Atheism, CRT, BLM, Racism, KKK, secular humanism, etc... are All the work of Satan. Hitler was a Darwinist. He believed there was a "Superior Race", and wanted it to be the German Race. He murdered not only the Jews but anyone who was handy-capped.

Karl Marx was a demonically controlled madman , possessed by Satan. He came up with Communism and Socialism ideologies to destroy people's ability to enjoy their lives, their freedoms, their God-Given liberties, their talents and abilities, etc... and force them to submit to wicked government control of every area of their lives. Anyone who opposes the Communist Government is put into prison, tortured and murdered. Sometimes the Communist Government of China even harvests the organs of the people they murder. The Government Demands to be "God" and refuses to allow the real God of Heaven and Earthy to be Freely Worshipped.

THE MEDIA'S HATRED IN AMERICA

The Satanic media has not stopped spewing it's lies, false accusations, name calling, deceptions, and hatred for anyone who tries to follow Jesus. The media attacks anyone who wants school prayer, wants the Bible taught in the schools and colleges, wants conservatism, values, morals, the real history of our Nation taught, the Christian Faith of the Founders of our Nation taught etc. The media is against righteousness, honesty, integrity, love, joy, peace, gentleness, patience, kindness, morality, truth, Biblical Values, obedience to God, the worship of Jesus, and God's Commandments and God's Words.

The media puts out lying stories and false narratives to deny truth, cover up for criminals by blaming other innocent people for what the guilty have done, and attacks anyone who does not agree with their Satanic lies and wicked, Marxist agendas. They censor out anyone who would tell the truth about anything. If people only hear the media's lies and never get to hear the truth, they will believe the lies. They are keeping people from hearing all sides of every issue so they can make right decisions about what they believe. They are indoctrinating people, especially children and teens, into horrible, lust and perversions that the Word of God says are , "Abominations." If our children become like Sodom and Gomorrah, God will destroy them. Even the children of Sodom and Gomorrah were filled with lust and sexual sins, and perversions. They were destroyed along with their parents, by God. Do we want our children and future generations to be atheists and devil worshippers? Do we want them thrown into hell for all eternity? Hitler said , "If we get them when they are young, we got them."

Genesis 2:26 "And God said, Let us make man in our own image, after our likeness: and let them have dominion over the fish of the sea, and over the fowl of the air, and over the cattle, and over all the earth, and over every creeping thing upon the earth." The "us", is the Trinity: God the Father, God the Son (Jesus), and God the Holy Spirit. He is One God in three persons.

Genesis 2:27 "So God created man in his own image, male and female created he them." Only human beings are created in God's Own Image in the wombs of their mothers. We have a physical body, a soul (emotions, feelings, and a will), and a spirit (a heart area to love or hate, forgive or not forgive, choose to do good or evil). We are a trinity.

No fish, bird, or animal (including apes) , are created in the image of God. Only human beings are created by God, in God's own image. Satan hates God.

Satan Hates People and wants to destroy as many human beings as he can. He uses the media as a vessel to promote his bitterness, unforgiveness, hatred, violence, riots, etc...deliberately turning groups of people against each other in order to destroy people, made in the image of God. Anyone harboring hatred, bitterness and unforgiveness, in their heart, is serving Satan and not the God of Love. Repent, surrender it to God and ask God to help you to forgive and love others.

Just as the wicked media dehumanized the Jews in Germany, and the Tutsis in Rwanda and Burundi, the wicked media has dehumanized sixty-two million innocent, unborn babies, and put them to death. For every baby that has been murdered, generations of human beings will never be. Satan has destroyed billions of human beings, made by God in the image of God , through abortion.

Jesus tells us in John 8:44 that Satan is a murderer from the beginning and the father of lies. Anyone who tells lies to murder innocent people, is a child of the devil. Satan is the murderer and the liar.

The Word of God makes it clear that God forms people in the womb of their mothers. A babe is a human being at conception. Even most biologists have agreed to that fact.

Luke 1:41 "And it came to pass, that, when Elizabeth heard the salutation of Mary, the babe leaped in her womb; and Elizabeth was filled with the Holy Ghost." Notice the "babe" was in her womb. The child was NOT A BLOB OF TISSUE, NOT A PRODUCT OF CONCEPTION, and NOT A FETUS. Women give birth to human babies.

Jeremiah 1:4-5 Then the Word of the Lord came unto me saying, "Before I formed you in the belly I knew you; and before you came forth out of the womb I sanctified you, and I ordained you a prophet to the nations."

Psalm 139:13-17 (King James Bible) David said to God, "For you have possessed my reins: you have covered me in my mother's womb. I am fearfully and wonderfully made: marvelous are your works: and that my soul knows right well. My substance was not hid from you when I was made in secret, and curiously wrought in the lowest parts of the earth. Your eyes did see my substance, yet being unperfect; and in your book all my members were written, which in continuance were fashioned, when as yet there was none of them. How precious also are your thoughts toward me, O God!"

Notice that God planned him (wrote what he would look like, his talents, his gender, his abilities, his eye color, his skin color, his hair color etc...), in a book and then fashioned him according to God's plan for his life. God does that with every baby He is creating in the womb of their mother.

Our Bill of Rights, in America says, "All people are created by the Creator for life, liberty and the pursuit of happiness." Where does the Creator (God), create life? In the womb of their mothers. Babies don't just pop out of the air. Storks don't bring them. They are created by God in the womb of their mothers for a right to life. Abortion is Un-Constitutional. Wicked, Satanic judges have decreed the murders of millions of people that God (the Creator) was creating in the wombs of their mothers, for His Divine Plans and Purposes.

Abortion denies babies their right to life. The very first right anyone can have is a right to life. It is the basic right of every human being. Without living, we cannot pursue liberty or happiness.

One of God's Commandments is, "Thou shall not kill (murder)." So why are we murdering innocent babies and claiming to be Christian? Only a Satanist or a deceived person, would want to destroy innocent human beings made in the image of God. Only a Satanist would want to cut up human beings into pieces, sell their body parts to wicked scientists for experiments with rats, and shed innocent blood to anger the God of Heaven. When Cain murdered Abel, Abel's blood was crying out to God from the ground. Can you imagine how much innocent blood is crying to God for justice; from garbage dumpsters, abortion clinic floors, unmarked graves, scientist laboratories, etc? We must stop this devil worship now!

In the Old Testament, all the false god worship involved the shedding of innocent blood and child sacrifice to devils and demons, along with all kinds of sexual sins and perversions. Children were burnt in the fire- forced to go through fire, by their own parents and burnt to death. Children were murdered and put into the gates of their parents properties to appease their devil gods.

When is this Nation going to STOP WORSHIPPING BAAL AND SATAN? When are we going to VALUE ALL HUMAN LIFE THAT GOD HAS CREATED FROM THE WOMB TO "THE GRAVE? In a Nation that murders it's children - it's future generations and the elderly, is anyone's life really safe?

Save the dogs, cats, tigers, elephants, whales, and seals, and MURDER THE HUMAN BEINGS, MADE IN GOD'S IMAGE, BY THE CREATOR OF THE UNIVERSE? This insanity must stop now. All Human Life Must be Protected Now, both in the womb and out of the womb, from conception to the grave.

America, Stop Murdering Your Children and Your Future, in Jesus Name. Amen!

There are two things that need to happen. Our youth need to stop having sex outside of marriage. If they stop it, they won't get pregnant, get VD, get Aids, get other diseases, get hurt, get used, get sexually abused, etc...

Adoption must be made less costly and easily available to married couples. Many married couples, who cannot bear children and want children, cannot afford the expensive fees involved in "Adoption." If the fees were taken away, they could adopt these babies and raise them. The babies would have a chance to live, walk, go to school, see a flower, a sunrise, a bird, enjoy a life and have parents to love them and raise them.

A baby is a baby in God's sight. He does not call them dehumanizing names such as "fetus", "blob of tissue", "a Product of Conception", etc... " The fruit of the womb is Jesus's reward," the Bible says.

The media and Planned Parenthood never tell the truth about the women who have suffered emotionally, physically, and spiritually from an abortion. There is a link between breast cancer and abortion. Having an abortion gives a woman a higher risk of breast cancer. They never tell you that.

Some women, after an abortion, will never be able to carry a baby full term. Their insides got damaged. Some women have died having so called "legal abortions." The clinic workers drive the women to the hospital so their death is recorded there and not at the clinic.

They never show the women the ultra sound of their babies. They look at the ultra sound image to figure out how big the babies head is so they will know what to charge them for the abortion. They don't show the women their babies, because if they did , most of the women wouldn't abort them.

The abortion known as "partial birth abortion", is a full term abortion that actually risks the mother's life. The baby is turned from a normal birth position head down, to a feet first position (a breech birth) so they can pull the baby's feet out first and stab the baby in the head before the head is delivered. Our Senate voted to stop partial birth abortion and Bill Clinton vetoed it and allowed it to continue. The innocent blood of these babies is on his wicked head.

Now, these wicked Satanists want to be able to murder babies who are out of the womb for a month. Month old babies are now deemed not worthy to live, if the parents decide they don't want them. Let someone else have and raise the child, if you don't want it. When will the Satanic Slaughter of Innocent Blood Stop in Our Land? When will people rise up and demand it to stop now? How many more innocent human lives will be destroyed by Satan and his followers? Haven't they murdered enough innocent people? Will they start murdering two and three year old children next? Will you be next on their demonic hit list? God Forbid!

During Covid 19, people, who were sick with Covid 19, were deliberately placed in nursing homes to infect and murder the elderly. There were beds in many other places But They Deliberately put the Covid 19 infected people into wards in the nursing homes to expose the seniors, make them sick, and murder them.. They murdered about 40,000 senior citizens. Who will be targeted next by these maniacs?

The media lie of "White Privilege", is another ridiculous , lying bit of nonsense. Anyone I know, who owns a house, has worked hard for years to pay the mortgage, pay the taxes, pay the repair bills etc... No one gave them their house. They worked hard for what they have. No one gave them any "freebies", "free land", "free houses", "free cars", or anything free. Whether they are white, black, brown, Oriental, Hispanic, etc.. They worked hard for years to pay for their houses. Anyone who wasn't lazy and worked hard could apply for a loan and purchase a house. No one was privileged or treated better than anyone else. When will the lying media tell the truth?

Anyone who owns a business, worked hard for years, took out loans to purchase the merchandise to get started and has paid the bank for years. No one gave them their businesses. They worked hard for what they have. No one has the right to burn businesses, put people out of work, and attack people who work hard and earn a living. The lazy people who refuse to work should not receive any "Freebies", at the expense of hard working American people. Enough is enough! They have nothing because they are lazy and won't work. God blesses the work of our hands. He doesn't bless laziness and slothfulness. Get a Job!

Enough of the Lawlessness of the Wicked Politicians, the Wicked DOJ, the Wicked FBI, the Wicked Marxists, Communists, Socialists, Darwinists, Satanists, Witches, Wizards, Evolutionists, Wok, CRT, BLM, KKK, Nazis, haters of God, haters of people, racists, haters of America, haters of our Freedom, Liberty and Justice, Our Constitution etc.... May the Lord put a speedy end to them and their wicked plans, plots, schemes, and agendas, in Jesus Name. Amen! May God's Executed Judgment come upon them suddenly and may we see their evil faces no more, in Jesus Name. AMEN!

The battle for your soul, for your family, for your freedoms, for your rights and liberties, rages on. The Battle for the very heart and soul of America and it's people rages on. Will it be Jesus (Yeshua), Father God, and Holy Spirit? Or will it be Satan and his kingdom of darkness and wickedness that you serve?

Will you serve the God of truth, righteousness, love, peace, joy, gentleness, patience, kindness , light, and life? Or will you serve the fallen angel, Satan, whose hates you, hates God, hates Jesus, hates truth, hates mankind, and whose destiny is the lake of fire?

Read Revelation 20:10? Will you wind up thrown into the lake of fire, because you chose to serve Satan and not Jesus? In Revelation 20:15, "And whosoever was not found written in the book of life was cast into the lake of fire."

When we read Revelation 21, it describes the new heaven and the New Jerusalem. It is beautiful. In verse 27, it says, "And there shall in no wise enter into it anything that defiles, neither whatsoever works abominations, or makes a lie: but they which are written in the Lamb's Book of Life." The Lamb is Jesus. When a person receives Him, their name is written in His Book of Life. People who reject Him, are not in the Book of Life and cannot enter the New Jerusalem. They are cast into the lake of fire. That will be the fate of the wicked people, if they continue to serve Satan and not God.

Serve Jesus and have eternal life in heaven to look forward to.

In Mark Chapter 8:36, Jesus asks, "For what shall it profit a man, if he shall gain the whole world, and lose his soul?" What good is it if you gain money, fame, fortune, and everything this world has to offer, and lose your eternal soul? Eternity is forever and forever, and forever. This short life on earth is temporary. To live a selfish, Godless life on earth , and burn in hell and the lake of fire, is a ridiculous choice.

Sadly, many people are blind to eternal things and they don't consider where they are going , when they die. They live only for the here and now and forget they will give an account of their life, to God. They serve the God of greed, the love of money which is the root of all evil, and everything else evil, wicked, and wrong. They choose to reject

God, His Word, His Son, His Holy Spirit, His Truths, His Instruction , His Love, His Peace, His Joy, His Righteousness, His Kindness, His Goodness, and Heaven. By their own free-will, they willingly reject the God that Created them. It is sad to see them throw their lives away and end up in hell instead of heaven ,forever.

Make the right choice. Choose to turn to Jesus today. Be among the ones that know Him, are written in His Book of Life, and can enter the New Jerusalem. Today is the day of Salvation. Tomorrow may not be yours. Do it Now.

CHAPTER 15
TRUST IN THE LORD
WITH ALL YOUR HEART

In Matthew 10:37-40, Jesus said, "He that loves father or mother more than me is not worthy of me: and he that loves son or daughter more than me is not worthy of me. He that does not take up his cross and follow me, is not worthy of me. He that finds his life shall lose it; and he that loses his life for my sake shall find it. He that receives you receives me, and he that receives me receives him that sent me."

If we truly love Jesus, He will be Number 1 in our hearts and lives. We will trust Him and surrender our entire lives to Him, allowing Him to lead us into Father God's Will and Purposes. God's Plans for you are far greater than any plans you could possibly make for yourself. Just Trust Him, Surrender Fully to Him, and see the amazing things He will do in you and through you. You will become His Hands and His Feet to touch many lives for Him. Your Destiny, in Jesus, is Huge if you give Him your entire life. Serve Him fully. Trust your life to Him. He Loves You!

In Mark 8:34-38, Jesus says, "Whosoever will come after me, let him deny himself and take up his cross, and follow me. For whosoever will save his life will lose it but whosoever shall lose his life for my sake and the gospel's, the same shall save it. For what shall it profit a man, if he shall gain the whole world; and lose his own soul? Or what shall a man give in exchange for his soul? Whosoever shall be ashamed of me and my words in this adulterous and sinful generation; of him also shall the Son of Man be ashamed when he comes in the glory of his Father with the holy angels."

If we look at what the Apostle Paul says in Galatians 2:20-21, it will help us to understand what Jesus meant. "I am crucified with Christ: nevertheless I live; yet not I, but Christ lives in me; and the life which I now live in the flesh I live by faith of the Son of God, who loved me, and gave himself for me."

Paul was saying, I am dead to my own will, my own plans, my own agendas, myself and my life. Christ is the Lord of my life. Christ is the one leading this life, which belongs to Him. He lives in me. I live by faith in Jesus, who loved me and gave Himself for me. Jesus is living this life, in me, and through me to do Father's Will, not my will. Jesus is Lord of this Life.

Have you ever repented of doing your own will and not God's Will? Have you ever given yourself and your entire life (every area of your life), to Jesus? Do you trust Jesus with your entire life-your family, your finances, your children, your future? Do you believe that God has big plans for your life? He won't show you what He has for you until your fully surrender to Him. You won't know God's Plans until you surrender your plans.

> In Matthew 12:48-50, Someone told Jesus that his mother and brethren were outside. Jesus said, "Who is my mother? and who are my brethren? And he stretched forth his hand toward his disciples, and said, "Behold my mother and my brethren! For whosoever shall do the will of my Father which is in heaven, the same is my brother, and sister, and mother." What about the people who don't surrender and do Father's Will? Are they really related to Jesus?

There are many people, in the Body of Christ, who run around trying to do "things for God." They need to pray, surrender to God, find out His Will, line up with Him, and do the things He directs them to do. Many people are wasting their lives doing all kinds of things God has not called them to do. Unless they surrender their lives fully, seek God, ask Him to direct their steps; they will never fulfill the reason and purpose He created them for. It is very sad.

A Christian woman was laying in a hospital bed, dying of a brain tumor. She said, "I wish I had done more for Jesus. I wish I had more time to make a difference in this world, for Jesus. It's too late for me now." Don't die with rue and regrets. Line up with God's Plan and Purpose for your life. Surrender fully to Him and let Him live in you and through you. You will be amazed at what He enables you to do and accomplish.

God's Plans are so big, you cannot accomplish them without Him. If He has called you to do something, trust Him, stop making excuses, step out in faith, and begin. He has already prepared you, anointed you, trained you, and given you what you need to do it. Be led by Holy Spirit and Step Out in Faith, as Holy Spirit leads you. Obey Holy Spirit. He is The part of the Trinity that is here now, on planet earth, to help us, guide us, teach us, comfort us, etc...The Power to Preach the Gospel of Jesus Christ, heal the sick, raise the dead, deliver people from demons, bind up the broken hearted, comfort the hurting, etc... comes from Holy Spirit. He is the indwelling Holy Spirit mentioned in John 14;12-17. Let Him operate in you and through you.

Pray and repent of doing your own will. Surrender your entire life and will to Jesus today and ask Father God to show you His Will and His Purpose for your life. Trust Jesus with every area of your life, including your life itself. Hold nothing back and see the Amazing Things God Will use you to do.

He is Bigger than any Mountain, Bigger than any Obstacle, Bigger than any Power, Bigger than any Principality, Bigger than any Devil, Bigger than any Demon, Bigger than the Grave, Bigger than Death, Bigger than anything or anyone else, and Bigger than Satan himself. Satan is just a fallen angel that rebelled against God. God created the angels.

Jesus is the REAL GOD! HE is the Creator of Everything Seen and unseen. He created the galaxies, the solar systems, the planets and their orbits, the birds of the air, the fish of the sea, the mammals on planet earth, the sun, the moon, the stars, the seas, and all nature. There is no mother earth, but we do have a Father God.

God created man in His own image, to fellowship with Him. He desired a people who would return His love and be part of His Spiritual Family. He is the Real God of Heaven and Earth. Read the Bible. Get to Know Him, love Him, worship Him, and obey Him. He loved you enough to suffer for you, to take your punishment for sin upon Himself so He could forgive and pardon you. He died a horrible death in your place; so you could be forgiven. He overcame death when He Rose From the Dead, came out of the grave, was seen by over five hundred people alive, before He ascended back up into heaven. HE LOVES YOU. HE DESIRES A LOVE RELATIONSHIP WITH YOU.HIS NAME IS JESUS!

ACCREDITATION

The Bill of Rights and the Constitution were mentioned and some passages were quoted.

All scripture verses were taken from the Thompson Chain Reference, King James Bible. Please note that for clarities sake, some of the verbiages have been changed to current day English. For example, "thee", to you, "harken" to hear, "Behold" to see, etc…

All word definitions were taken from Websters New World College Dictionary, Fourth Edition.

The reference to Plymouth Colony, came from an excellent book entitled, "The Pilgrim Chronicles" An eyewitness History of the Pilgrims and the Founding of Plymouth Colony, by Rod Gragg.

The reference to the Azusa Street Revival came from the book, "Azusa Street They Told Me Their Stories", Foreword by Billye Brim and Storyteller Tommy Weichel printed by Dr. J. Edward Morris and Cindy McCowan.

All references to Communism, socialism, Marxism, the persecution of Christian believers, and communist activities here in America and around the world came from many articles from the Epoch Times Newspaper and The Voice of The Martyrs publications as well as Nora Lamb Ministries.

THANK YOU

First, I thank my Jesus for loving me and saving me from myself and the devil. I thank Father God for sending Holy Spirit to convict me of my sinful, lost state and drawing me to Jesus. Thank You Jesus for loving me enough to take my punishment, for my sins , upon yourself. Thank You for paying for my sins with your own sinless blood. Thank You for the Great Salvation, Deliverance, and Healing that you purchased for me and for the human race.

I want to thank the two men who prayed for my salvation and led me to faith in Jesus Christ. If it wasn't for them, I would probably be in hell right now.

A special thank you to my Husband Paul and Son Brian, who funded my Africa mission trips, and other mission trips. They sacrificed, so that I could leave home for weeks at a time to serve the Lord.

Last of all, I want to thank everyone who loves Jesus, follows Jesus, and serves Jesus; with all of their hearts, minds, souls and strengths. Thank You for your dedication, sacrifices, loyalty and love for God and His People, and the Lost Souls. May you hear Jesus say to you, "Well done My Good and Faithful Servant", in the day you see Him face to face, in Jesus Name. Amen!

9 781964 097299